Cage Of Iron

Douglas Fulthorpe

SILVERMO☽N
PUBLISHING

www.silvermonpublishing.co.uk

© 2012 Douglas Fulthorpe

SILVERMOON
P U B L I S H I N G

A Division of Silvermoon Productions Limited
3rd Floor I 207 Regent Street I London I W1B 3HH
0207 096 0979
www.silvermoonpublishing.co.uk

ISBN 978-1-910457-21-4

Silvermoon Publishing is an innovative publishing house established to publish plays and license rights to theatre companies world-wide. Silvermoon aims to promote its plays and playwrights to ensure that its playwrights get maximum exposure.

VIDEO-RECORDING OF AMATEUR PRODUCTIONS

Please note that the copyright laws governing video-recording are extremely complex and that it should not be assumed that any play may be video-recorded for whatever purpose without first obtaining the permission of the appropriate agents. The fact that a play is published by Silvermoon Publishing does not indicate that video rights are available or that Silvermoon Publishing control such rights.

PERFORMING LICENCE APPLICATIONS

A performing licence for these plays will be issued by "Silvermoon Publishing" subject to the following conditions:-

1. That the performance fee is paid in full on the date of application for a licence.
2. That the name of the author(s) is/are clearly shown in any programme or publicity material.
3. That the author(s) is/are entitled to receive two complimentary tickets to see his/her/their work in performance if they so wish.
4. That a copy of the play is purchased from Silvermoon Publishing for each named speaking part and a minimum of three copies purchased for backstage use.
5. That a copy of any reviews / Marketing materials be forwarded to Silvermoon Publishing.
6. That the Silvermoon Publishing licensing statement be displayed on any marketing material.

FEES

Details of script prices and fees payable for each performance or public reading can be obtained by telephone to (+44) 0207 096 0879 or to the address below. Alternatively, latest prices can be obtained from our website. www.silvermoonpublishing.co.uk.

To apply for a performing licence for any play please write to Silvermoon Publishing, 3rd Floor, 207 Regent Street, London W1B 3HH or email via our website with the following details:-

1.   Name and address of theatre company.
2.   Details of venue including seating capacity.
3.   Dates of proposed performance or public reading.
4.   Contact telephone number for Author's complimentary tickets.

Or apply directly via our website at www.silvermoonpublishing.co.uk

PROFESSIONAL RIGHTS

Professional rights should be addressed to Silvermoon Publishing.

DOUGLAS FULTHORPE

Douglas Fulthorpe has been writing science fiction and macabre and humorous fiction for a while. After winning the second and third prizes in the American National Fantasy Fan short story contest, he had three short stories read on the BBC North Region, one published in the sf magazine Vision of Tomorrow, five in Science Fiction Monthly, one of which, The Death Of Man, was feature story in the collection The Best Of Science Fiction Monthly. Dummyblind was published in the American sf magazine Analog.

Recently he has had three satirical plays published by New Theatre Publications. He lives in his home town of Tynemouth, Northumberland, England.

His short story, Afternoon Tea, was published in The Journal in August 2011.

He has had two short stories broadcast on The South Tyneside Talking Newsletter.

His poem Ode To A Factory Toilet Monopoliser was published on-line in Inkapture. The presenter described it as "a very strange story," which made Douglas rather proud.

He has had several short stories and serious articles published in Author, the magazine of the British Civil Service.

ACKNOWLEDGEMENTS

The author is grateful for suggestions and advice regarding the impracticalities of mounting a full-size submarine on a small, provincial stage such as that of a church hall, and the difficulties in staging the vessel's submerging and surfacing, especially in view of the ever-increasing cost of water.

It was reluctantly decided also to abandon plans to include full-scale naval ordnance and torpedoes, particularly following advice from the Royal Society for the Prevention of Cruelty to Animals, which pointed out that cats may, and usually do, sleep at any time of the day and night. Criticism and comments will be welcome, especially if written on the back of a postage-stamp, preferably unused.

Most of all, thanks are genuinely expressed for the essential and unstinted help received from friends, in areas of document format and preparation, theatrical presentation, and proof-reading.

AUTHOR'S FOREWORD

Cage of Iron was conceived on a northern beach in the early years of the Third Millennium. The notion took form gradually and tenuously during daily training stints, as thoughts and imaginings meandered in an ultimately successful attempt to ease the torture of placing one straining foot ahead of the other over five gruelling yet always enjoyable miles. Possibly a faint echo of the soul of a long-drowned submariner had drifted from a distant ocean, wandering with the currents from warm climes to vanishing ice-caps on a leisurely and tranquil quest for a resting-place. At last, the long decades of searching ended as a gentle tide bore it peacefully to sanctuary. Here, its memories were enabled to find expression....

I had long been a keen follower of theatre at all levels, from the pit to the gods. Through the course of all the drama, comedy, revues, monologues and farces there formed slowly a smouldering belief, conviction even, that I could write just as badly. Whether my dedication and perseverance in pursuit of that goal have brought success is not for me to judge. But at last the searing inferno within erupted in an incandescent shower, translated by charcoal wand onto flame-proof foil.

Cage of Iron is set in the later stages of the Second World War. The story begins in spring, 1943, shortly after the tide of war has turned against Germany, with the annihilation of the German Sixth Army by the Russians at Stalingrad, and the victory, on a far smaller scale of men and weapons, but of great strategical importance, of the British Eighth Army at El Alamein.

The tide has turned against the U-boats as well, yet U999 survives, following her erratic and usually misguided course through unlikely scrapes and mishaps to the very last moments of the war.

Although the play has its background in the armed services during the war, the intention is not to ridicule the Armed Forces, but to caricaturise the mistakes and blunders, both the comic and the tragic, which most, if not all, of us make throughout our working and private lives, while not neglecting the fine and noble acts which many individuals perform.

There is no intended message, save perhaps the oft-repeated, "expect to make mistakes," and the time-worn adage that heroism has a short span. Nevertheless, tribute is here made humbly to the volunteers of the Allied submarine services, and to those of the Kriegsmarine as well, who also fought and died for their country, albeit in a monstrously evil cause. Whatever their side, all were heroes.

CHARACTERS

All the main characters will be readily recognisable as "stock", clichéd even, stereotypes, gleaned from countless earlier films and novels: the incredibly stupid hero (Stollen), the beautiful woman flagrantly masquerading as a man, the strutting, fanatical Nazi, Frau Schulz, the "tart with a heart", the stupid and incompetent intelligence controller, and the somewhat dowdy, unfashionably dressed typist.. Even the ship's cat is a shadowy figure of enigma.

"U", LEUTNANT MULLER, a dedicated, yet compassionate, British Naval Intelligence Officer (Lieutenant Miller), who has infiltrated the German Naval Intelligence Service. As U999's Security Officer, he is at least as powerful as the captain. He is strikingly good-looking, with lustrous, dark and wavy hair, which is covered by his naval cap throughout the play (he even wears it when washing) until the final act. He then reveals to his unsuspecting comrades, what has been obvious to the audience from first sight, that he is a beautiful and sensuous woman.

KAPITAN STOLLEN, the commander of U999. He is a professional sailor and a patriot, but is deeply sceptical of Nazism. He is kind, handsome, courageous, and, on occasion, incredibly stupid.

LEUTNANT SCHLANGE, the first officer and second-in-command. He is known universally as "Snake", to which he answers cheerfully. He is a fanatical, somewhat excitable Nazi, dedicated to his Fuhrer, and is ready and proud to commit any betrayal or, indeed, atrocity, which will serve the interests of Fuhrer and Reich. He dreams of a career in espionage, and actually has a small network of contacts in Naval Intelligence. His perceived potential as a threat, as recognised by senior officers, has resulted in his secondment to a front-line U-boat. His bravery is not in question, and he shows commendable loyalty to his fellow-officers, and unflinching readiness to admit to his own mistakes.

"I". CAPTAIN CARSTAIRS. He is a capable, young, British Naval Intelligence officer, who, unknown to Lieutenant Miller, has also infiltrated German Naval Intelligence.

"O", COMMANDER MORRISON. A senior officer in British Naval Intelligence, his veneer of bluff and genial stupidity masks a core in which lurks an intermittently germinating grain of intelligence.

FRAU SCHULZ, the Hostess in Chief of the U-boat Officers' Home in Cuxhaven, She is a large, very attractive woman of forty, kind-hearted and cheerful, with more than a hint of wistfulness. She has lost whatever faith she once had in Nazism. Her "club" combines accommodation, games facilities, and rest-rooms, and also supplies the services of voluntary hostesses for the officers.

PETTY-OFFICER SCHMIDT, a petty-officer on U999.

REAR-ADMIRAL SCHLEIM, a senior officer in German Naval Intelligence. As the occasion demands, obsequious or coldly arrogant; his aim is to survive.

MISS MILLBANK, an attractive, if somewhat dowdy, secretary-typist in British Naval Intelligence.

ADOLF HITLER, self-styled genius and first Fuhrer of the Third Reich.

EVA BRAUN (HITLER), his devoted friend, admirer and, finally, wife.

TOM (UNSEEN), U999'S CAT. Is he a British master-spy or just a devoted mouser, toiling for his bowl of cream and a sardine or two? Does he even exist?

Act 1, Scene 1

Spring. 1943. The control-room of U999, somewhere in the North-Atlantic. In the cramped space are the periscope, a clock, multitudes of gauges and dials, control-wheels and levers, a maze of pipes and cables, the torpedo-launching controls and various items of machinery. In the middle and at rear is the periscope; to its left is a ladder leading up into the conning-tower. There is a small locker (which later houses a manual and recognition booklet) by the periscope. A door at back-left leads off forward, and at front-right is the door to LEUTNANT MULLER's cabin. This is also on set, and is visible to the audience. It contains simply a bunk and a wash-basin with mirror. A curtain in a corner covers a "wardrobe". There is also a small cupboard, set in the bulkhead. During Act 1, and subsequently, alternate halves of the set are blacked out as required.

A faint oil-haze is discernible in the ghostly half-light of the control-room. The muted hum of the electric propulsion motors is present continually. The backdrop above the control-room is dark.

Introductory music, fading after half-a-minute or so, is "Wooden Heart", played as a military march.

KAPITAN STOLLEN and LEUTNANT SCHLANGE are standing by the periscope, with PETTY OFFICER SCHMIDT at the controls. He is not visible to the audience. SCHLANGE is bearing a Luger automatic, which he carries at all times.

STOLLEN:	(*wrinkling his nose*) Gott im Himmel, this cursed chlorine is pretty bad today. Better have the Electrical Officer check the batteries for leaks before you go off, Snake. (*Looks at the clock.*) Which should be in about three minutes, when Leutnant Muller relieves you.
SCHLANGE:	Do you know anything about him, Kapitan? He has been onboard for two weeks, but has said nothing about his background.
STOLLEN:	Well, he graduated with good marks from the academy. We met on the quayside at Cuxhaven, as he was coming to join us. He had spent a year training in Naval Intelligence. He said he would be glad to get to sea, because his parents had died in a fire-storm when Hamburg was bombed. Understandably, he does not appear to want to talk about his background.
SCHLANGE:	I can see why. I will speak to the Electrical Officer, Kapitan.
STOLLEN:	We should be near our hunting-ground by now. (*He smoothly raises the periscope.*) Black as night.
SCHLANGE:	Permit me, Kapitan. (*He slides the periscope cover to one side and the backdrop changes to a dim grey.*)
STOLLEN:	That's better. (*He scans the scene for about thirty seconds.*) Nothing there but thick mist. It needs watching, though. Take over, Snake.
SCHLANGE:	(*watching intently*) I thought I saw something. It's gone. (*A faint, shadowy shape appears briefly, then fades. Then, abruptly, the dark silhouette of a gigantic battleship fills the backdrop.*)

SCHLANGE:	Ja, it is there. I see it. We must fire.
STOLLEN:	What is it?
SCHLANGE:	A British battleship.
STOLLEN:	Here, alone? It is unlikely. Here, give it to me. (*He motions SCHLANGE to one side. The shape disappears.*) There is nothing there.
SCHLANGE:	I tell you, Kapitan, it was there. The mist has swallowed it.
STOLLEN:	Pshaa! A trick of the mist, or perhaps I should halve your daily rum ration.
SCHLANGE:	(*indignantly*) I tell you it was there, Kapitan; I saw it quite clearly.
STOLLEN:	Rubbish. (*The shape reappears. In a surprised tone*) Hallo, now I am seeing things.
SCHLANGE:	Kapitan, may I see?
STOLLEN:	(*thoughtfully*) Surely we can't both be seeing things. Maybe I should call the Medical Officer.
SCHLANGE:	Kapitan, the Medical Officer is on shore in Cuxhaven. May I have a look? (*He takes the periscope, and peers intently. The ship fades.*) We have lost it again. (*The ship reappears.*) No, there it is, unmistakable!
STOLLEN:	Unmistakably what, man?
SCHLANGE:	Unmistakably the Duke of Cornwall, Britain's latest and most secret battleship. So secret, in fact, that they have not even told their own fighting personnel yet. The crew believe they are on a pleasure-steamer.
STOLLEN:	That makes sense. Does Berlin know?
SCHLANGE:	Only a few at the top know.
STOLLEN:	Why haven't we been told?
SCHLANGE:	Because High Command in Berlin has not made up its mind on how to let us know without tipping off the British that we know too.
STOLLEN:	So how do you know?
SCHLANGE:	(*still peering intently*) I have a (*hesitates*) acquaintance in High Command who tells me everything. It is definitely the Duke of Cornwall... (*Shrieking*) Kapitan, we must attack!
STOLLEN:	Stand aside. Yes, it is much clearer now. Interesting; they fly the British naval ensign; a far more attractive flag than that silly crooked cross of ours. (*Ruminatively*) So redolent of history and world-wide traditions. You know, I remember our history teacher saying to me---
SCHLANGE:	Kapitan---
STOLLEN:	(*genially*) Of course not, dummkopf. How could he? I was just an urchin in a cute little brown shirt and miniature jack-boots.
SCHLANGE:	(*shrieking*) Kapitan, it is an enemy ship. Kapitan, please!
STOLLEN:	(*shaking himself*) Himmel! Action stations!

SCHLANGE moves to the torpedo-launcher. Simultaneously the klaxon sounds loudly and continuously; there are several bangs and the sound of running feet. LEUTNANT MULLER's door opens, and LEUTNANT MULLER dashes in, buttoning his tunic and adjusting his cap.

MULLER:	What is happening?

STOLLEN:	(*Still at the periscope*) A British battleship. Prepare to launch number one torpedo!
MULLER:	Let me see! I must see! (*Looks briefly through the periscope.*) Do not fire! Oh, the Fuhrer's stars must be watching over us today, to avert such a calamity.
STOLLEN:	Fuhrer's stars; what are you babbling about?
SCHLANGE:	The Fuhrer is a passionate believer in astrology. And so am I. If it is good enough for our beloved Fuhrer, then it must be right.
STOLLEN:	Yes, yes. (*Impatiently*) Leutnant?
MULLER:	(*without turning from the periscope*) Schweinhund!

STOLLEN and SCHLANGE gasp and stare speechlessly at each other.

STOLLEN:	Repeat that!
MULLER:	(*still at the periscope*) Schweinhund!
STOLLEN:	Leutnant, are you mad?
MULLER:	(*turning to STOLLEN and SCHLANGE*) You fools; do you want to end up in a concentration-camp? Don't you recognise one of our own Schweinhund-class battleships?
SCHLANGE:	(*aghast*) Kapitan, the Leutnant is wrong. He is the Security Officer, but I am fully trained in ship-recognition. Our Schweinhund ships have a completely different silhouette, and she flies the British ensign. That is the Duke of Cornwall. We must attack!
MULLER:	(*returning to the periscope*) Yes, I see the British flag; the mist is clearing and I can also see plainly the dummy superstructure. I am sure she is on a secret mission, probably penetrating the River Thames to bombard Buckingham Palace. That would end the war at a stroke, if the British lost their beloved King George and Queen Elizabeth. (*Slowly*) Yes, I am sure it is a German battleship in disguise; a master-plan of our glorious Fuhrer.

SCHLANGE has a disbelieving look on his face.

STOLLEN:	Hmm. Let me see. It certainly has British camouflage.
MULLER:	Part of the plan.
SCHLANGE:	(*shrieking*) It is definitely a British battleship.
MULLER:	Do you want to risk killing two thousand of your comrades?
SCHLANGE:	(*gazing open-mouthed at MULLER*) Kapitan you must arrest the Leutnant.
STOLLEN:	(*glancing around*) Why is that?
SCHLANGE:	He has just accused me of being a spy.
STOLLEN:	I didn't hear that. What makes you say that?
SCHLANGE:	They are not my comrades. They are British: I am German.
STOLLEN:	(*Turning to MULLER*) You're the Security Officer. Can I arrest you?
MULLER:	No.
STOLLEN:	Did you accuse him of being a spy?
MULLER:	(*considering the situation thoughtfully*) Yes, I suppose I did.
STOLLEN:	Then he must stand trial.
SCHLANGE:	Kapitan, while we argue, the ship is getting away.
STOLLEN:	(*taking another look through the periscope*) No, she is still there. Interesting; there are two searchlights on the bridge,

	sweeping the ocean. (*Two searchlights shine from the ship for a minute or so.*)
MULLER:	Probably rehearsing some sort of tableau they will project onto the Tower of London, before they blow Buckingham Palace off the face of the Earth.
SCHLANGE:	(*despairingly*) Kapitan.
STOLLEN:	(*turning from the periscope*) We must have a drumhead court-martial. Schmidt!
SCHMIDT:	(*offstage*) Kapitan.
STOLLEN:	Tell the ship's bandmaster I need his drum.
SCHMIDT:	Kapitan, the band is rehearsing for tonight's dance in the forepeak They will be at least half-an hour.

On the backdrop the battleship looms, its searchlights flashing and sweeping intermittently.

STOLLEN:	We can't wait that long. It is afternoon-tea in half-an-hour, and the cook is serving his speciality; fried schinkenwurst with ersatz chocolate sauce produced from Silesian brown coal. (*To the audience*) I think I should jump ship. (*Motioning to SCHLANGE*) Pass me that drum. Schlange picks a metal drum, which he sets down, revealing the letters, WC.

STOLLEN is about to sit on the drum, then he notices that it is open-end uppermost. He smiles, then inverts it.

STOLLEN:	(*sitting on the drum*) Thanks. Now I need a judge's cap. I'll have that (*pointing to a rating's cap on a console. He puts on the cap. It has two black ribbons, which hang over his forehead.*) I had better be jury as well. (*To MULLER*) Paper.
MULLER:	(*horrified*) Paper, Kapitan?
STOLLEN:	Of course; for trials notes.
MULLER:	Oh, I see. (*He picks up a large book clearly labelled "LOG", then tears out a sheet and hands it to STOLLEN.*)
STOLLEN:	Thanks. Actually, I do need a tissue.
MULLER:	(*goggle-eyed*) Kapitan? (*He hands a tissue to STOLLEN.*)
STOLLEN:	Thanks. (*Wiping his nose, then pointing at SCHLANGE's pistol*) Give me that.
SCHLANGE:	Why?
STOLLEN:	As executioner, I might need it. (*SCHLANGE reluctantly passes over the pistol.*)
STOLLEN:	(*to MULLER*) Now, how do you plead?
MULLER:	Not me, Kapitan; him.
STOLLEN:	(*to SCHLANGE*) Well?
SCHLANGE:	Not guilty.
STOLLEN:	Why did the Leutnant accuse you of spying?
SCHLANGE:	He said the Britishers on our target were my comrades.
STOLLEN:	I don't understand. Why would Berlin crew one of its battleships with Brits?
MULLER:	Kapitan, we don't say that yet. You mean, Britishers.
STOLLEN:	(*to SCHLANGE*) Well?
SCHLANGE:	Kapitan, it is not a German ship. It is a British battleship. I am not a spy.
STOLLEN:	Good. Case dismissed, but I find you guilty of dereliction of

	duty by time-wasting, and I am minded to punish you with the utmost severity. (*He glances at the pistol.*)
MULLER:	(*hastily*) That will not be necessary, Kapitan.
STOLLEN:	(*judicially*) I see. Then what do you suggest?
MULLER:	(*considering*) The Leutnant could be confined to the ship for the duration of the voyage.
STOLLEN:	Harsh, but necessary. Sentence decreed. (*He hands the pistol back to SCHLANGE.*)
SCHLANGE:	(*imploringly*) Kapitan, please look at the target again.
STOLLEN:	(*looking through the periscope*) The searchlights are still sweeping, and what are all those men doing at the stern? Now they are launching objects into the air.
MULLER:	They are probably rehearsing some entertainment for the stupid English. What is that Scottish game? Of course, tossing the haggis.

Abruptly there are flashes of light near to the bows and the stern.

STOLLEN:	Now there are lights flashing.
MULLER:	Signals, no doubt. Probably God Save the King. (*Hastily*) I would not signal back, though.

Suddenly there are deafening detonations, the control-room shakes, and the lights flash rapidly on and off several times before the room is plunged into darkness.

After a lengthy pause, the lights go on again. SCHLANGE is picking himself up from the deck. He has fallen headfirst against a console, and his face is bleeding. STOLLEN is lying spread-eagled across MULLER, who has his arms around him. SCHMIDT has been blown out of his cubicle, and is on his knees. Water is jetting into the room at several points. They pick themselves up.

STOLLEN:	Dive--dive--dive! Stop engines! (*He rapidly lowers the periscope, while the other three race around, frantically spinning wheels, pulling levers and tripping switches. After half-a-minute they pause. SCHMIDT goes back into the cubicle.*)
STOLLEN:	What is the depth, Schmidt?
SCHMIDT:	(*offstage*) Forty metres and falling, sir.
STOLLEN:	Down to two hundred metres.

More detonations follow, but greatly muted. SCHLANGE, who is sitting at a control-desk, with hydrophones on his head, wrenches them off with a curse. The engines have stopped and the submarine is deathly quiet.

STOLLEN:	(*turning to SCHLANGE, who has put the hydrophones on again*) Anything?
SCHLANGE:	Not a sound, Kapitan.
STOLLEN:	Either we have lost them or they have stopped their engines and are playing cat and mouse. So we wait, and we keep silent. Not one word. And don't even use the toilet. (*Considers.*) If you must, be discreet.

Half-an-hour passes.

STOLLEN:	Maintain two-hundred metres. Snake, start the engines. Two knots steady. Absolute silence.

SCHLANGE turns a wheel, and the faint hum of a motor is heard. Darkness falls slowly over the control-room.

Act 1, Scene 2

LEUTNANT MULLER's cabin. The door opens and MULLER enters. After a cautious look behind him he goes to the wall cupboard and lowers the door, revealing a radio-transmitter. He sits at the radio and presses a key. A call-signal is heard, and is repeated twice. Suddenly there is a crackle of static, then a voice is heard. Simultaneously, in the darkened part of the stage, CARSTAIRS' head and shoulders appear in half-light: he is sitting at a radio-transmitter in London.

CARSTAIRS:	(*to melody, Indian Love-call*) When I'm calling you--oo--oo--oo--oo--oo--oo!
MULLER:	I will answer true--oo--oo--oo--oo--oo--oo. (*To melody, Carmen Miranda song*) Ay--ay--ay--ay--ay--I like you vairee much.
CARSTAIRS:	Ay--ay--ay--ay--ay--I think you're grand.
MULLER:	Agent U here.
CARSTAIRS:	Agent I here.
MULLER:	Well, we live to fight again.
CARSTAIRS:	Thank God. We have been trying to warn you all day that the Duke of Cornwall was in your vicinity, but you must have been submerged and could not hear us. They spotted a submarine four hours ago, and could not take a chance, so they attacked it.
MULLER:	That was us. I had to think fast or the Duke of Cornwall would be among the fishes now.
CARSTAIRS:	What did you do?
MULLER:	I fooled the Captain into thinking it was a Schweinhund-class ship in disguise.
CARSTAIRS:	(*disbelievingly*) And he believed you?
MULLER:	Eventually. We have just had quite a discussion. The Captain wanted to know why a German ship should open fire on us. I said it was because they could take no chances, and would assume we were British. I reminded him that we, the Germans, that is, have a long tradition of flying false colours in order to fool our enemies; something the British are too stupid to do. Schlange liked that, but he said he still believed it was a Royal Navy ship.
CARSTAIRS:	What about the Captain; did he accept that?
MULLER:	Yes. He believed me, but said that we must report everything that had happened. I pointed out that Berlin would not be pleased on learning that we had almost sunk the Schweinhund, and then I asked them, did they want to go to a concentration-camp, or to be shot? Stollen said, "Do we have a choice?" Schlange said that, if he had made a mistake, he would happy to die to atone for it. I pointed out that he could hardly serve his Fuhrer from the grave. He became thoughtful at that, but the Captain said, nevertheless we must report faithfully what had happened.
CARSTAIRS:	Damn. I still think he must be very stupid.
MULLER:	Actually, he is, but quite nice with it.
CARSTAIRS:	Hey, don't go soft on him.
MULLER:	(*reacting hotly*) Of course not! That Schlange, or Snake,

	as everyone calls him is the one to watch, though. He really lives up to his nickname.
CARSTAIRS:	Do you think perhaps he is there to spy on you?
MULLER:	He thinks he is. (*Thoughtfully*) I'll have to watch him, though.
CARSTAIRS:	We've got to do something. Once the German naval command reveals that there was no Schweinhund-class ship in the area, your goose is cooked. Have you radioed in to Berlin yet?
MULLER:	No. I've managed to convince the Captain that we must maintain radio silence so as not to jeopardise Schweinhund's secret mission. But there is the ship's log to worry about, and I will have to submit an incident report, countersigned by the Captain, by hand to Berlin. That is the order, whenever we are engaged in any kind of action.
CARSTAIRS:	That need not be a problem. We have managed to infiltrate a first-class man, Agent R, into the Berlin structure. He personally presents all reports to the High Command. He will substitute a fake report for yours, somewhat modified, saying you were attacked by an unidentified British battleship, with no mention of Schweinhund. We will back it up with an announcement that our forces sank a U-boat, suitably vague, of course, to make them think we have something to conceal. That should do the trick. Who compiles the ship's log?
MULLER:	The Captain and I.
CARSTAIRS:	When does it go in for routine inspection?
MULLER:	Not for another six months.
CARSTAIRS:	Can you alter the log by then?
MULLER:	No doubt. I am well trained in that sort of thing.
CARSTAIRS:	Good. You were chased by an unidentified British battleship.
MULLER:	Will do. Agent U signing off.
CARSTAIRS:	Agent I signing off. Good luck! (*He fades from the stage.*)

MULLER straightens up and closes the cupboard-door, then stifles a yawn and stretches his arms out, before going to a wash-basin and mirror, which faces the audience. Without removing his cap, he peels off his jacket, then unbuttons his shirt and slides it back over his shoulders, revealing a very attractive back. He then lays the shirt on a chair beside him.

There is a knock on the door, which opens simultaneously, and KAPITAN STOLLEN enters.

STOLLEN:	Leutnant--(*he breaks off and stares with surprise at MULLER's bare back. MULLER looks at STOLLEN's reflection in the mirror for a split second, their eyes meeting, then he whips his shirt on, quickly buttons it, dons the jacket and turns around, hastily buttoning as he does so.*)

The pair stand transfixed, staring wide-eyed at each other.

Act 2

6.30 pm, late November 1943. The lounge of the U-boat Officers' Home in Cuxhaven, which provides accommodation and various forms of recreation for officers of the U-boat service.
There is a door from outside at front right. Another door, further back, gives onto LEUTNANT MULLER's room. There is an open door at the back, leading on into the club, from which music, conversation, the clinking of glasses and laughter can be heard. The atmosphere of the lounge is one of warmth, comfort, and relaxation, befitting men who have endured months of danger and extreme hardship at sea. There are tables, chairs, a settee, armchairs, a radio, gramophone, and a well-stocked bar.
FRAU SCHULZ is standing in the middle of the silent room. She is fortyish, has upswept hair, and is strikingly attractive. She is wearing a sleek dress (crimson, emerald or pale blue satin), displaying shapely shoulders and a hint of copious bosom. She stands for some time, with her hands crossed before her, looking wistful, as though reliving past times.
She closes the door into the club, cutting off the sound, then crosses quietly to the gramophone, absently takes a 78 rpm record from a small table, and places it on the turntable. Immediately the loud strains of the Horst Wessel song fill the room. The expression drains from her face as she recoils a pace or two, then she folds her arms, and stands regarding the gramophone with distaste for thirty seconds.
She removes the record, replaces it on the table, and carefully selects another record. Softly, the theme from the Threepenny Opera begins.
FRAU SCHULZ sits on a settee and wipes a tear from her eye.
Short pause.
LEUTNANT MULLER enters from outside. The music fades.

FRAU SCHULZ: *(rising with a pleased expression)* Leutnant, how delightful to see you again.

MULLER: *(throwing off his greatcoat but leaving his cap on)* And you.
They shake hands.

MULLER: *(rubbing his forearms)* It's cold out there.

FRAU SCHULZ: Never mind, it's warm as toast in here. How are you?

MULLER: Pretty good. How are you?

FRAU SCHULZ: Wunderbar! Your room is prepared for as you, as usual.

MULLER: Of course. *(Casually)* Any news? Two months on a U-boat leaves you quite out of touch. *(Archly)* I know you wouldn't reveal anything too sensitive.

FRAU SCHULZ: *(shrugging)* You are right. It doesn't pay to talk too much. We are told that the war is going well, but I keep on noticing that some of our boats are not returning to Cuxhaven. Maybe they have been transferred to other bases. And so many new faces in the crews of the replacement boats.
Some of the men coming from leave tell me that the cursed Tommies are getting more audacious with their raids on our cities. It is time that Reichsmarschall Goering gave them another Coventry.

MULLER: I am sure he plans to do so soon. Well, I have just travelled to Berlin and back and I am looking forward to a bath and a night

	in bed in a real room, instead of a tin can, so I will bid you, "Guten Abend". (*He turns to go.*)
FRAU SCHULZ:	Leutnant. Have your bath and a rest by all means, but wouldn't you consider joining us?
MULLER:	Of course. (*Laughs.*) I could do with a change of company. But right now I need sleep.
FRAU SCHULZ:	Fine. (*Smiling*) Some of the girls are very interested in you. (*Laughs.*) They think you are quite different.
MULLER:	(*recoiling slightly*) Oh!
FRAU SCHULZ:	(*anxiously*) Leutnant, are you all right? You've gone quite pale. You had better sit down for a minute or two.
MULLER:	(*taking a seat on an armchair*) Just a little tired. (*Recovering*) I'll be fine.
FRAU SCHULZ:	There's quite a party going on next door. It got a bit boisterous, I'm afraid, so I came out for a few minutes. And of course we have the cinema, an exercise-room, and a library containing only approved books. Really, after six months at sea I would expect you to need a little (*pauses.*) pleasure. At least have a drink before you go.
MULLER:	(*brightening, with a very English accent*) Thanks, I would like a gin and it, or a gin and French
FRAU SCHULZ:	What are those? I have never heard of them.
MULLER:	Gin and vermouth.

FRAU SCHULZ raises her eye-brows, looking puzzled, then mixes a drink and hands it to MULLER.

MULLER:	And yourself?
FRAU SCHULZ:	Why not? I'll have the same. (*Pours a drink, then sits on a settee, facing MULLER. They each take a sip.*)
MULLER:	(*relaxing*) This is better than that tin-can with its stink of diesel-oil, chlorine, human sweat and excrement, the endless rattle of the motors and the perpetual, glaring lights. And our boys dying in the darkness and the cold, one hundred fathoms down, and those poor devils on the blazing oil-tankers or exploding ammunition-ships. Not that I have seen any, thank God.
FRAU SCHULZ:	(*sadly*) So much has changed.

The light fades. When it returns, FRAU SCHULZ is sitting alone on the settee, with her drink in her hand.

KAPITAN STOLLEN enters and looks at FRAU SCHULZ .

STOLLEN:	Are you all right? (*He takes off his greatcoat and cap. FRAU SCHULZ takes them and hangs them on a coat-stand.*)
FRAU SCHULZ:	Yes, I'm all right. A drink, Kapitan; beer or schnappes?
STOLLEN:	I think I would rather just sit. (*He sits down.*)
FRAU SCHULZ:	Kapitan, I suppose that Snake fellow will be in soon.
STOLLEN:	I expect so. (*Looks enquiringly.*)
FRAU SCHULZ:	It's just; he makes me shudder. Nobody likes him.
STOLLEN:	(*reasonably*) I cannot stop him from coming here. His life is very hard, and he is an extremely capable officer.
FRAU SCHULZ:	And all this Sieg Heiling and saluting every five seconds.
STOLLEN:	(*laughing*) You should have seen him when he first came aboard; Heil Hitlering; saluting and stamping his feet all the

time. He even bashed the periscope in one of his more energetic salutes, and smashed a knuckle. (*Laughs.*) We had to tell him to stop finally, in case the Tommies heard him. (*Sighs.*) I would like to say, they broke the mould when they made him, but, unfortunately, there are many more like him. (*Shakes his head.*) Some of the fellows have a crucifix above their bunks; he has a swastika.

FRAU SCHULZ: (*nods resignedly; cheerfully*) Some female company, perhaps? Any of the girls would be happy to sit with you. You could watch a film, talk, or whatever.

STOLLEN: No the girls are all very nice, but their company is not what want tonight. I really need some time to get away from that (*pauses.*) different world on the U-boat.

FRAU SCHULZ: I understand.

STOLLEN: And that's not all. (*Hesitates.*) I've been rather (*pauses.*) disturbed lately.

FRAU SCHULZ: Haven't we all?

STOLLEN: (*hesitating*) It started soon after Leutnant Muller came aboard. (*He pauses, then exhales heavily.*) I can't sleep, can't concentrate, and when we are together--frankly, my feelings alarm me. Some time ago I saw him in his cabin, and--(*breaks off and stares ahead.*)--I talk too much. (*He lowers his head.*)

FRAU SCHULZ: (*jocularly*) So you don't want my young ladies. Does nobody want my girls? (*Laughs.*) Don't say you want me! (*She breaks off abruptly, crimsoning, then stands up, holding up her hands. She stares at STOLLEN in horror.*) Oh no, Kapitan, do you mean what I am thinking?

STOLLEN: (*slowly*) I don't know what I mean.

FRAU SCHULZ: I will never repeat one word of what you have said. That is a criminal offence, for which you could end up in Dachau or worse. (*Hoarsely*) For God's sake, man, think about girls, think about me, yourself, football, anything, but forget the Leutnant. (*Sound of door closing.*) Ach! Someone comes.

LEUTNANT SCHLANGE strides in. He is not wearing a greatcoat, but has a swastika armband on his sleeve, and is bearing his pistol. He keeps his cap on. FRAU SCHULZ slumps onto the settee, and KAPITAN STOLLEN picks up a newspaper and opens it on his lap.

SCHLANGE: (*rubbing his arms vigorously, then clicking his heels and giving the Nazi salute*) Heil Hitler!

FRAU SCHULZ: (*giving the Nazi salute and speaking half-heartedly*) Heil Hitler!

STOLLEN intently studies his newspaper.

SCHLANGE: (*turning to FRAU SCHULZ; brusquely*) Heil Hitler!

FRAU SCHULZ: (*rising to her feet, saluting energetically, and speaking with forced conviction*) Heil Hitler! (*Remains standing uncomfortably.*)

SCHLANGE: That's better. (*FRAU SCHULZ sits down. Turns to STOLLEN. Pointedly*) Heil Hitler!

STOLLEN: (*studying his newspaper, without looking up*) Hello, Snake. What do you fancy for the two-thirty at Potsdam?

SCHLANGE: Kapitan, I said "Heil Hitler!"

STOLLEN:	(*still looking down*) What about Eastern Runner?
SCHLANGE:	(*gazing at him fixedly for a few seconds*) Kapitan, your attempt at humour is questionable.
STOLLEN:	(*without looking up*) Who's joking? It's a racing certainty.
SCHLANGE:	Do you mean what I am thinking?
STOLLEN:	That's the second time someone has said that to me tonight.
SCHLANGE:	It is very dangerous to talk in such a fashion. (*Breathes hard.*) I am aware that there have been (*hesitates.*) delays on the Eastern Front, but the Fuhrer has said that the conclusion is inevitable.
STOLLEN:	(*drily*) Very.
SCHLANGE:	(*angrily*) Men have gone to concentration camps for far less than what you have said tonight.
STOLLEN:	(*setting his newspaper aside*) Yes, that is true, but you may have noticed that more and more of your comrades are going to watery graves---
SCHLANGE:	There is not, and has never been, a shortage of volunteers for U-boat Command.
STOLLEN:	Very true, and no-one can ever deny their courage, but we cannot easily replace trained men. It takes a long time to train an officer, and, sad to say, time is another thing which the Fatherland is lacking.
SCHLANGE:	(*now ice-calm*) Kapitan, I have seen that you are a courageous man, and, until you got that knock on the head when the torpedo fell on you, a first-class commander, but have a care. The Third Reich will only tolerate so much, and I have influence in Berlin.
STOLLEN:	Why the armband, anyway? Are you going to a parade?
SCHLANGE:	I find I get more respect when I bear the Party armband.
STOLLEN:	Don't you get enough respect just by wearing your naval uniform?
SCHLANGE:	When I wear the armband, people tend to be more attentive. They listen when I speak to them; argue less; open doors; give way for me.
STOLLEN:	Sounds like fear.
SCHLANGE:	Perhaps, but that is not my motive. Vanity does not come into it, and I have no great desire to see people cowering before me, but in the armband they see the symbol and authority of the Deutsches Reich. Therefore, when the need arises, they will be obedient in serving and meeting the needs of the Reich, with neither question nor hesitation. That is the way of the Reich. (*Turns to FRAU SCHULZ; politely and quietly*) Frau Schulz. (*Bows.*)
FRAU SCHULZ:	Herr Leutnant.
SCHLANGE:	Call me "Snake". (*Turns to go, and, over his shoulder, casually*) Have Monika come to my quarters.
FRAU SCHULZ:	(*straight-faced*) I am afraid that will not be possible, Herr Snake.
SCHLANGE:	(*turning around to face her*) Just Snake, if you please. Why not?

FRAU SCHULZ: Monika won't be in tonight. She is not so well.

SCHLANGE: That's all right; Delphine will do.

FRAU SCHULZ: She is having a night off.

SCHLANGE: Then make it Greta; she is pretty good.

FRAU SCHULZ: She is visiting her parents in Klagenfurt.

SCHLANGE: Monika is sick; Delphine is not coming in; Greta is in Klagenfurt. Isn't there anybody?

STOLLEN: (laughing) It seems they will not jump for your armband, Snake.

All three actors break off, exchange meaningful looks, and smile.

SCHLANGE surreptitiously pulls a scrap of paper from his pocket, studies it briefly, then mutters to prompt.

PROMPT: (*loudly*) Poses stiffly!

SCHLANGE snorts and suppresses a laugh. FRAU SCHULZ laughs outright. They come to order.

SCHLANGE: Frau Schulz?

FRAU SCHULZ: Leutnant, I don't know how to say this, but I must be truthful. All the girls are at the dance. (*Hesitates.*) Leutnant, none of the girls is really comfortable with you. You are a volunteer, like everyone else in U-boat Command---

SCHLANGE: It so happens I did not volunteer. Alone in U-boat Command, I am here by direction.

STOLLEN sits up in surprise.

FRAU SCHULZ: (*with dignity*) I was about to say, the girls are also volunteers. They are not your common Reeperbahn whores. If you want those, go to the ratings' brothel around the corner. These are young ladies from good Aryan stock, members of the League of German Maidens, who have come here out of a sense of devotion to the Reich, to bring some comfort to the heroes of the Kriegsmarine. But they have threatened to walk out rather than to go to you.

SCHLANGE goes to the bar, pours himself a large glass of schnappes, then sits in an armchair, laying his cap on the arm of the chair. He takes a leisurely drink, then stretches his legs out.

SCHLANGE: (*calmly*) I will tell you how I came to be known as Snake. It was nineteen-thirty-three, and our Fuhrer had not long been elected Chancellor of Germany. I was ten years old, and at the local Lutheran church school. We were all regular churchgoers; father, mother, myself and my sister, who is now serving loyally as a supervisor at a labour-camp in Jersey.

STOLLEN: Is she in the SS?

SCHLANGE: (*glancing at STOLLEN, but continuing*) One day our pastor was invited to take a group of us to a Party Rally. He agreed readily, since his predecessor had been removed from office for conduct unhelpful to the Reich.

The Fuhrer's first words were electrifying. "Deutschland awake!" he said, then paused, at which point we prodded awake those who had drunk rather too much of the schnappes which the Hitler Youth had been slipping us.

I listened spellbound as he spoke--some unkind journalists wrote, "raved"--for two hours, enunciating his vision of a

world-wide Reich. He spoke with burning zeal of our honour, privilege, and duty to strive unflinchingly in the face of all obstacles, which our enemies would employ, towards that goal. When he finished, the applause could be heard sixty kilometres away in the Harz Mountains.
From that moment my sole and total commitment in life was to serve without question and tirelessly my Fuhrer, the Party and Germany.

STOLLEN: (*folding his newspaper and setting it aside*) Snake, we were all hoodwinked. (*FRAU SCHULZ nods agreement and folds her arms.*)

SCHLANGE: (*zealously*) Not hoodwinked. As the Fuhrer urged, awoken. Not long afterwards, my father was unwise enough to switch off the radio when the Fuhrer was about to speak. I told him, that if he ever again showed disrespect to our Fuhrer, I would report him to the local Gestapo. Later he was induced to join the Party, and became an enthusiastic member. (*Seriously*) And he is, to this day, very grateful. He has told me several times that he will never forget what I have done.

STOLLEN: (*rising*) I think I will go and watch a film.

FRAU SCHULZ: I will join you, now that we know why they call you (*looking at SCHLANGE*) Snake.

SCHLANGE: (*motioning them to remain seated*) No, hear my story. (*As his "story" unfolds, the lights progressively dim somewhat, while a moderate spotlight shines on him.*) On my first day at the Hitler Youth Camp, I caught the decadent Commandant performing a disgusting act---

FRAU SCHULZ: I don't want to hear this. (*She and STOLLEN nevertheless stare with interest and revulsion at SCHLANGE.*)

SCHLANGE: I had him arrested for listening to, and actually enjoying, a degenerate record of jazz: South Rampart Street Parade. (*Laughs softly.*) Now he parades in Buchenwald. I was immediately transferred to the School of Naval Intelligence. There I was, in Bad Oder.

STOLLEN: (*nodding in agreement*) And not for the last time.

SCHLANGE: (*motioning with his half-full glass*) A drink? Come on; three comrades sharing a drink together. (Smiling) Come on, Kapitan; surely you will drink with a fellow Atlantic veteran?

STOLLEN: (*hesitating, then slowly*) I'll have a schnappes.

FRAU SCHULZ: I'll have the same. (*She gets to her feet.*)

SCHLANGE: (*draining his glass and motioning to FRAU SCHULZ to remain seated*) No, no. (*He pours three drinks, and hands two to his companions. He sits down, visibly relaxing.*)

SCHLANGE: (*smiling*) Even the most dedicated servant of the Reich needs rest and recuperation.

STOLLEN: What happened next?

SCHLANGE: (*raising his glass*) Prosit!

STOLLEN and SCHULZ: (*together*) Prosit! (*All three drink.*)

SCHLANGE: (*enthusiastically*) During my time at the Naval Academy, I was living my dream. From the first moment, in every course, task, lesson and exercise, it was as though someone was in my mind, guiding me and telling me what to say and do. I rapidly mastered every technique known: surveillance, telephone-tapping, espionage, lip-reading, suspect interrogation, assassination, seduction, drugs--everything. The instructors said I was a natural.

And I was not slow in applying what I had learned. By the end of the first year I had my own intelligence network in the school. No file was secure from me; no lock could defeat me. The knowledge I gained gave me great power over my fellow cadets, and with it came respect, which in turn, although I did not seek it, brought popularity. Someone jokingly called me "Snake", and the name has endured. I graduated one year early, with the highest mark ever achieved. At passing-out the Commandant described me as unique; without parallel in his experience.

You can imagine my astonishment and consternation when I was marched off the camp under SS guard to join a U-boat. I still remember the send-off I had from my fellow cadets, who lined the route and clapped and applauded me to the gate. (*Appreciatively*) Some even gave the Nazi salute as I passed. I have spent a lot of time trying to fathom the reason for my assignation, and I still don't know. However, I believe it was because of orders from above.

(*He drains his glass, and gets to his feet, picking up his cap.*) Now, Frau Schulz, you may accompany me to my quarters.

FRAU SCHULZ: (*rising slowly and with great reluctance, extreme revulsion on her features, while STOLLEN watches straight-backed and wide-eyed; after a long pause*) Leutnant Schlange, there have been occasions on which I have accepted invitations, assignations even; on others I have declined, but to associate with you would be like consorting with your namesake. Now, you can have me sent to the Eastern Front, from which Hilda, whose parents live in Frankfort an Oder, tells me there are endless processions of trains bearing wounded troops, or to one of the concentration-camps which you are so proud of. Either one would be preferable to sleeping with you.

SCHLANGE: (*very calmly to FRAU SCHULZ*) I found out that one of my fellow cadets had a slight blemish in his ancestry; enough to cause him serious problems if it were to be disclosed. He is now in Berlin HQ, working for me. And there are others. It would quite easy for me to have your records modified, with perhaps a false caution in your past. Have a care. (*He turns and walks off slowly through the door at rear to his quarters. STOLLEN and FRAU SCHULZ stare after him.*)

STOLLEN: Well... The whole world needs to have a care, with that fellow.

He takes a sip of schnappes. FRAU SCHULZ sits down heavily and takes a gulp from her glass.

The door on the left opens and LEUTNANT MULLER walks in.

MULLER: What was all that about? (*Glances at FRAU SCHULZ.*) I was

	just dozing off when I heard him going on.
STOLLEN:	That's all right. You can speak in front of Frau Schulz.
FRAU SCHULZ:	You should be careful, Kapitan. There are spies and informers everywhere.
MULLER:	Very true.
STOLLEN:	It was just Snake telling us how popular he is and how he was the best ever cadet at Bad Oder Academy.
MULLER:	(*laughing*) And that's why he is on a U-boat.
STOLLEN:	Frau Schulz, would you get the Leutnant a drink, please.
FRAU SCHULZ:	Leutnant?
MULLER:	Schnappes will be fine, thanks. (*FRAU SCHULZ gets her a drink.*)
STOLLEN:	You must have been at the academy when he was there. Did you know him?
MULLER:	(*casually*) No; actually, I was at a different school.
STOLLEN:	Oh, where was that?
MULLER:	On a remote headland near Konigsberg.
STOLLEN:	Interesting; I grew up near Konigsberg. Where was it?
MULLER:	It was a very obscure spot; very secret.
STOLLEN:	Hmm.
FRAU SCHULZ:	After all that, I think I am ready for bed. (*Laughs.*) On my own. If you need anything, just ring for the maid. Guten Abend!

STOLLEN and MULLER: (*together*) Guten Abend!

There is a long pause after FRAU SCHULZ leaves. Embarrassed and clearly ill-at-ease, they avoid looking at each other.

MULLER:	(*awkwardly*) Well, the incident report has gone in.
STOLLEN:	(*embarrassed*) Good, good.

Another long silence.

MULLER:	(hesitantly) Kapitan….
STOLLEN:	Yes?
MULLER:	As you know, I was seconded to U999 to gain first-hand experience of U-boat operations to assist me in my work with Naval Intelligence on shore.
STOLLEN:	Yes, well at least you have seen life at the sharp end.
MULLER:	And the blunt end.
STOLLEN:	(*sipping his drink*) Not to mention the middle.
MULLER:	(*nodding*) My six-months' secondment will soon be over.
STOLLEN:	(*pauses for some time, then, sipping schnappes, slowly*) I will not oppose it, of course, and on your performance to date my Captain's report will cause you no problems--quite the contrary. You have proved yourself a first-class officer in every respect. It's funny, though…

MULLER looks enquiringly.

STOLLEN:	Things are definitely getting worse. The Allies have got radar now, and you're just patrolling on the surface, or giving the lads a well-earned breath of air, when out of the sun comes a Catalina or a Sunderland flying-boat, strafing you with cannon or depth-charges. And they seem to know so much of our actions. Do you think they could have cracked our code?
MULLER:	(*thoughtfully*) It certainly is an enigma.

STOLLEN:	(*glancing at MULLER*) That's the name of our code. It's impossible, though; they can't have broken it.
MULLER:	Ever thought of asking to transfer ashore?
STOLLEN:	Not I. I am a volunteer, and I am not ducking out now that things are getting tough.
MULLER:	They might not let you go, anyway, and , come to think of it, I might be kept at sea. Losses are mounting, and, although new U-boats are rolling off the stocks, trained crews are not easily replaced. I will just have to wait and see.
STOLLEN:	I was thinking how strange it is that, since you came on board, we have not had one sighting of an enemy ship. Not that I think you have brought us bad luck. Without your intervention we would have sunk a Schweinhund-class battleship. When they read the Incident Report, they could well shoot me for my stupid mistake.
MULLER:	Kapitan, both sides keep making mistakes like that. And visibility was really appalling that day. And, after all, the ship was disguised as the Duke of Cornwall. Soldiers shoot down their own aeroplanes; the RAF has dive-bombed Allied shipping, and the troop-carrier Queen Elizabeth cut the cruiser Curacao in half. No-one was shot for that, and we do not execute soldiers for mistakes; only for cowardice. No-one could accuse you of that.
STOLLEN:	We shall see.
MULLER:	Let's drink to future victory!
TOGETHER:	(*clinking glasses*) To victory.

Act 3, Scene 1

January 1944. The control-room of U999, in the Bay of Biscay. The oil-haze is visible in the glaring half-light, and the hum of the electric motors is heard. STOLLEN is gazing intently through the periscope, while SCHLANGE is making notes from gauge readings. MULLER is sitting, studying a manual. The backdrop displays a white-flecked, stormy sea under a grey sky. STOLLEN turns from the periscope, and looks around the control-room.

SCHLANGE:	Anything, Kapitan?
STOLLEN:	Nothing. Course, Schmidt?
SCHMIDT:	(*from cubicle*) Two points west of south south-west, sir.
STOLLEN:	Revolutions and inferred speed, Snake.
SCHLANGE:	Nine-hundred and sixty-eight, Kapitan, and eight knots.
STOLLEN:	And our last current estimate was two knots head-on. Estimated position, Snake.
SCHLANGE:	Ay, sir. (*He makes brief pencil calculations, then uses a slide-rule. Finally he picks up a chart, then draws a cross on it.*) Kapitan. (*He hands it to STOLLEN.*)
STOLLEN:	Excellent. Roughly two miles to the meeting-point. Prepare to surface. Muller!
MULLER:	(*looking up from the manual*) Yes, sir. I've been through it twice; all fifty thousand pages: there are no flaws. Every last, minute detail is pin-pointed; our course, the tonnage of the gold-bullion, details of the box seal, photographs of our contact-ship, and, most importantly, the identification code words, which only you know, Kapitan. (*He gets up and places the manual in a small locker beside the periscope.*)
STOLLEN:	Yes, most important. They will be very wary of possible attack by a British submarine, so we've got to get it right. I don't want those six-inch guns converting U999 into a colander. (Looks through the periscope.) Yes! Surface! (*A small, distant image of the side view of a ship is visible on the back drop.*)
SCHMIDT:	Surface it is, sir.
STOLLEN:	Kill the electric motors. Start the diesels. (*As SCHLANGE and MULLER run around, spinning wheels and pulling levers, the electric motor hum fades, and the clatter of the diesels takes over.*)
STOLLEN:	Full speed ahead.
SCHMIDT:	Full speed ahead it is, sir.

On the backdrop the image of the ship grows until it is big and quite close. The ship is a large freighter, pitching somewhat in the wild sea. There is a centre-castle and slender funnel, from which a plume of black smoke drifts in the wind. Two guns are visible on each well-deck. The blue and white Argentinean flag flies at the stern.

STOLLEN:	Snake.
SCHLANGE:	Kapitan.
STOLLEN:	You and Muller get up top and man the signal-lamp.
SCHLANGE:	Ay, sir. (*He and MULLER don oilskins, then SCHLANGE unfastens the hatch at the base of the conning-tower. A bucketful of water drenches him. Undeterred, he and MULLER*

	clamber up the ladder. The shrieking of the wind and the roar of the sea are heard.)
SCHLANGE:	(from deck) Cover is off the lamp. Ready to signal.
STOLLEN:	Flash the light.
SCHLANGE:	Signalling. (A light flashes on the freighter's bridge.) She's flashing back, "hot."
STOLLEN:	Good. Signal back.
SCHLANGE:	(shouting over the wind) Kapitan, is "hot" the right signal?
STOLLEN:	I'll check. I wrote it down somewhere. (He spots something on the floor by the periscope, bends down, then straightens up, holding a large flatfish, which he examines with interest.)
SCHLANGE:	(urgently) They're flashing again, Kapitan. (Light flashes.) They are flashing continuously, and the gun-crews are in position.
MULLER:	Kapitan, "hot" is the correct signal. What do we reply? (The shrieking of the wind intensifies.)
STOLLEN:	(laying the fish down; calmly) Now, I remember. I wrote it down on the back of my Spot the Ball entry for the Berlin and Bremerhaven game. Now, where did I put it? (Checks his pockets.) Who won that game, anyway?
SCHLANGE:	They're flashing again (light flashes.) "hot" and I can see the gun-crews making ready. The reply, Kapitan. Is it "cold"?
STOLLEN:	Don't ask me. You're up there.

There is a flash from one of the freighter's after guns, and, simultaneously, a deafening boom. The control-room shakes.

SCHLANGE:	Dog?
STOLLEN:	No need to be offensive, Leutnant.
MULLER:	Kapitan, it is "chili".
STOLLEN:	I know it is chilly. It is the middle of winter. (Laughs.) Leutnant, you trained on the Baltic coast. Surely you can stand a bit of cold. (He resumes searching his pockets.) Just hang on.
MULLER:	Snake, flash, "chili". It's our last chance.
SCHLANGE:	Signalling, "chili".

There is a pause, then the freighter's signal-lamp flashes back.

SCHLANGE:	(shouting) Hot chili.
STOLLEN:	(pulling a piece of paper from his pocket and studying it.) That's right. Hot chili. (He turns the piece of paper over and looks closely at it.) I wonder if I won.
SCHLANGE:	They're launching a boat, sir.

There is a crackle from the intercom.

RADIO OPERATOR:	(on intercom) Signal coming through, Kapitan.
STOLLEN:	Put it on.
STAGE-GERMAN VOICE:	(from intercom) Breaking radio silence briefly. This is the German naval ship Caramba, sailing under the Argentine flag. Happy to meet you , U999, although you gave us an anxious time there. Prepare to transfer cargo. (Through the moaning of the wind the "put-put" of a launch's motor is heard, growing louder as the launch approaches.)
SCHLANGE AND MULLER:	(together) Heil Hitler!
THIRD VOICE:	(from deck) Heil Hitler!
STOLLEN:	Down here, Snake. You and Schmidt begin transferring the

cargo. Muller, get the crane ready.

SCHLANGE AND MULLER: (*together*) Ay, Kapitan.

SCHLANGE descends from the conning-tower, then he and SCHMIDT, who has emerged from the cubicle, go to the door at the rear and open it. A packing-crate with two rope, lifting handles, no larger than a small suit-case, lies just beyond the doorway. The two men lift it, and clearly find it very heavy. They struggle with it to the base of the conning-tower. A rope sling with two hooks is lowered. STOLLEN attaches the hooks to the handles of the crate.

SCHLANGE: (*calling*) Heave up!

There is a whirr of a motor, and the crate ascends out of sight. There follow various bumps and mild, good-humoured curses.

THIRD VOICE: Lower away.

The set gradually darkens, then, after a pause, slowly becomes light again. SCHLANGE and SCHMIDT are struggling to carry a heavy crate to the conning-tower. STOLLEN attaches the sling-hooks.

SCHLANGE: Heave up!

The motor whirrs, and the crate ascends. A couple of bumps are heard.

THIRD VOICE: Lower away.

Pause.

THIRD VOICE: 'Wiedersehen!

MULLER: 'Wiedersehen!

THIRD VOICE: Heil Hitler!

MULLER: Heil Hitler!

MULLER: (*after pause*) Boat casting off with cargo, Kapitan. (*The fading "put-put" of the motor is heard through the shrieking of the wind.*)

STOLLEN: Stay up there, Muller.

MULLER: Ay, sir.

STOLLEN: (*smiling, to SCHLANGE and SCHMIDT*) Well done. I'll address the crew after we set sail, and there'll be an extra ration of rum, chocolate and cigarettes all round. (*Ruminatively*) All those crates of gold bullion. How many millions of Reichsmarks?

SCHLANGE: A lot.

SCHMIDT: Permission to speak, sir.

STOLLEN: That's all right.

SCHMIDT: What can we be buying from Argentina, sir? We get all our food from the occupied countries, and there's nothing else.

STOLLEN: That's what I'm wondering.

SCHLANGE: I am (*pauses.*) informed that there may be something very secret being planned.

STOLLEN: Don't tell us.

SCHLANGE: I don't know anyway. However, the Fuhrer is a visionary, and who knows what farsighted plans he may be formulating.

MULLER: (*from deck*) Caramba is taking the boat on board, sir. (*On the backdrop, a signal-light flashes from the freighter.*) They are signalling, "'Wiedersehen".

STOLLEN: Signal back, then come down.

MULLER descends, then closes the conning-tower hatch. There is a deafening blast from Caramba's siren, then the freighter slowly begins to turn stern-on as she resumes her journey. The intercom crackles.

RADIO OPERATOR: Signal coming through, sir.

VOICE FROM INTERCOM: Breaking radio silence. Thanks U999, and Good Luck. Now, the ship's choir and band have something to say.

A military band strikes up, "It's a Long Way to Tipperary".

CARAMBA SHIP'S CHOIR:

It's a long way to Argentina.

It's a long way to go.

It's a long way to Argentina,

and we won't be steaming slow.

Goodbye, dear Fuh-rer.

Farewell, Eva Braun.

It's a long, long way to Argentina,

and we're com-ing down.

The song begins again, then slowly dies away as the image of the freighter diminishes and fades. SCHLANGE, STOLLEN, SCHMIDT and MULLER stand with linked arms, facing the audience, and smiling with satisfaction as the stage dims.

Act 3, Scene 2

One hour later. LEUTNANT MULLER is sitting at the radio in his cabin. The rest of the set is in darkness. He presses a key; there is a crackle of static, then the upper half of CAPTAIN CARSTAIRS appears in half-light in the darkened part of the stage. He is wearing British naval uniform.

CARSTAIRS:	When I'm calling you--oo--oo--oo--oo--oo--oo!
MULLER:	Ay--ay--ay--ay--ay--I like you vairee much.
CARSTAIRS:	(*smiling expansively*) It went like a dream. We steamed up on a fast minelayer disguised as an E-boat. We knew all the call-signals and codes, so they fell for it hook, line and anchor. Four of us got onto the bridge; the radio was immobilised, then, with a revolver pressed against the Captain's temple, and the minelayer's guns ready, it was all over. The German crew are now safely below deck, looking forward to a spell in a holiday-camp in Canada. For the duration of the war.
MULLER:	So it's off to Argentina now.
CARSTAIRS:	We meet up with a tender at a remote Argentinean bay, hand over the fake gold, then take off for Canada with the real stuff. Two hours into our voyage we send out a fake distress-signal, saying we have been torpedoed by an Allied submarine and are sinking. Amen!
MULLER:	Sounds good. What about the time-capsule?
CARSTAIRS:	That's been taken care of. "O" thinks your idea is brilliant and he is to recommend you for a medal when (*hesitates.*) when it's all over.
MULLER:	If I survive.

Act 3, Scene 3

Later in January 1944. Admiral Schleim's office in Naval Intelligence, Berlin. It is dominated by a large, colour portrait of Adolf Hitler. There is a door at the back of the stage, and another at the left. On the right ADMIRAL SCHLEIM is sitting at a large desk, in front of which there are three chairs. There is an intercom and a telephone on his desk. He is looking at some papers. There is a knock on the door on the right.

SCHLEIM:	(*looking up*) Herein.

The door opens and STOLLEN enters, followed by MULLER and SCHLANGE. MULLER is wearing his cap, and SCHLANGE is bearing his pistol. They line up at attention.

ALL THREE:	(*clicking their heels and saluting*) Heil Hitler!
SCHLEIM:	(*standing up and in turn saluting*) Heil Hitler! (*His voice is well-modulated; his tone is warm.*) At ease, gentlemen. (*He goes to them and shakes hands with them.*) Be seated; be comfortable. (*They sit and SCHLEIM returns to his seat*).
SCHLANGE:	Sir, permission to speak.
SCHLEIM:	(*smiling*) Of course.
SCHLANGE:	We are honoured to be received by you, Admiral.
SCHLEIM:	(*with a deprecatory wave*) Leutnant, the honour is mine. I am privileged to meet those who have rendered such service to the Fatherland. Don't look so serious. You are here to be awarded high honours, not to be shot at dawn. For your successful endeavours in the shipping of the gold bullion to the Argentine. For you, Kapitan, the Iron Cross, Second Class. For you, Leutnant Schlange, the Iron Cross, Second Class. (*Both men look proud.*) And for you, Leutnant Muller, the Iron Cross, First Class. The higher award is in recognition of your idea of the time-capsule. Although, happily, it was not called into operation, I can say that the Fuhrer himself is pleased. And there is more: you will all be suitably entertained for one week at a mountain lodge in the Bavarian Alps, with appropriate recreation following your rigours at sea.

SCHLANGE brightens appreciably; STOLLEN remains indifferent, while MULLER frowns.

	Now, if you are at all still apprehensive, I can set your minds at rest. You will find the Fuhrer, despite the enormous pressures he bears, a kind and generous man. Although he is unwavering in his dedication at every moment to the service of his country, he is never too busy to honour the heroes of the Reich.

The intercom on SCHLEIM's desk chimes softly.

SCHLEIM:	(*respectfully*) Schleim. (*He listens attentively.*) Jawohl. (*To the three*) Der Fuhrer awaits you.

STOLLEN, MULLER and SCHLANGE stand up. The lights dim, and a muted, choral hymn begins. They file with dreamlike slowness towards the door at rear, which, as the lighting dims, is gradually illuminated in shifting hues of misty white and pale and delicate blue. The door opens silently, and, as they file slowly from the stage, the lights fade.
Pause.

SCHLEIM's office, one hour later. SCHLEIM is reclining back on his seat, with his hands clasped behind his head, absently gazing at the facing wall. He is smiling contentedly. He gives a relaxed sigh and carries on studying the wall. The telephone rings and he picks it up.

SCHLEIM: (*cordially*) Schleim. (*He listens.*) Was? (*He sits bolt upright.*) Was ist los? (*He listens attentively, his demeanour rapidly becoming animated and alarmed.*) Repeat that! (*Interrupting*) Nein, nein, not that rubbish about excellency and your grave news. Get to the verdammt point! (*He continues to listen with a horror-stricken expression.*) What--? (*His colour deepens, his voice rising to a roar.*) Der Fuhrer---

FEMALE VOICE FROM THE INNER ROOM: Was?

SCHLEIM: (*regaining his composure with difficulty, pleasantly*) Everything is in order. (*He lowers his voice and speaks urgently into the telephone.*) Who else has seen it? Good. Don't mention it to anyone and get over here with it now. And hurry--schnell, schnell!

Act 4, Scene 1

Early February 1944; one hour after dawn. The control-room of U999. The U-boat is submerged and stationary; only the faint hum of electrical equipment can be heard. The backdrop is pale grey. STOLLEN is standing in the centre of the stage with his arms folded. He looks concerned. SCHLANGE is peering intently through the periscope. MULLER is moving around, checking gauges.

SCHLANGE steps back, pushes his cap back, then turns around and, slowly and expressively, shakes his head negatively.

STOLLEN:	(*quietly*) Take a look, Muller. (*MULLER takes up position at the periscope.*)
STOLLEN:	(*to SCHLANGE*) I cannot understand it. We were to meet with the fleet at dawn. We took our last sextant reading at fourteen-hundred hours yesterday, and from it we were able to pinpoint our position. Since then we have travelled submerged and have relied on our fixed course and calculated speed to get us to our meeting-point. (*To MULLER*) Anything showing?
MULLER:	Absolutely empty, Kapitan, and the visibility is good.
STOLLEN:	Let's have a look. (*He takes the periscope and carefully rotates it through its arc of vision.*) Hmm. Take over, Muller. And you (*to SCHLANGE*) get along to the Chief Engineer and tell him I want him to check his rev-counter again and the ocean current now, and to have another look at his calculations. I'll speak to Schmidt.

SCHLANGE departs through the rear door, and STOLLEN goes into SCHMIDT's cubicle.

STOLLEN:	(*from cubicle*) Let me see your course log.
SCHMIDT:	(*from cubicle*) Jawohl, Kapitan. Here it is.
STOLLEN:	You logged it every fifteen minutes. Spot-on every time. You're sure you read the compass right?
SCHMIDT:	Kapitan, I assure you I have maintained the course you ordered. There has only been the slightest flicker of the compass needle, and I corrected it instantaneously. See for yourself; the setting is unchanged.
STOLLEN:	Ach so. The problem clearly is not here. Carry on, Schmidt.
SCHMIDT:	Kapitan.

STOLLEN emerges from the cubicle.

STOLLEN:	(*to MULLER*) Anything?
MULLER:	(*without turning*) Nothing.
STOLLEN:	Damn.

The rear door opens and SCHLANGE enters, looking flustered.

SCHLANGE:	Kapitan, the Chief Engineer says he has checked his rev-counters several times, using stroboscopic and electronic pulse methods. He says the counters are accurate to one part in a hundred thousand. He insists that his calculations are correct. He has checked them several times, and the Second Engineer has also checked them.
MULLER:	(*without turning*) Current?
SCHLANGE:	That has been checked several times. There is virtually no ocean drift, and the situation has been unchanged throughout

	the night. He said he can detect any changes in current from the note of the engine, and there has been nothing. He told me his calculations are correct and that we are either at the appointed destination or you have taken the wrong course, unless the fleet has gone to the wrong point.
STOLLEN:	Did you ask him about propellor-slip?
SCHLANGE:	He has a precise figure for propellor-slip. They are brand-new propellors, since you broke the last two on the dock-gate at Cuxhaven (*STOLLEN gives him a baleful glare, but does not interrupt.*) and the slip is precisely known. When I asked him to check his calculations just once more, he threatened to brain me with a Stilson-wrench if I did not get out of his engine-room. Kapitan, I think you should speak to him.
STOLLEN:	(*taking a step back*) In view of what you have just said, I think I had better not. (*Exasperatedly*) So much for our super-duper week in the Bavarian Alps; hauled off the train half-way there and packed back to Cuxhaven. Now it seems we are lost. (*Sighs.*) Ah, well. Give Muller a break, Snake.

SCHLANGE takes over at the periscope.

STOLLEN:	I am puzzled. (*The other two nod in agreement. Alertly to MULLER*) We haven't got the wrong day, have we?
MULLER:	No, Kapitan. All three of us have studied the operational directive in detail. We have the right data, and we can only check our bearings from the stars, which have gone, or from the sun, which is skulking behind a cloud.
STOLLEN:	So the gold never reached Argentina. Our agent in London uncovered the truth. Shortly after leaving us with the gold, the Caramba encountered a British cruiser which knocked out our lads' radio with the first shot. Caramba fought back, but never had a chance and went down with all hands. The British knew that Caramba was carrying the precious cargo of bullion, so they came up with the idea of delivering fake, gold-plated bars of lead, then returning later to retrieve the gold through an underwater operation. Except that they were unaware of your time-capsule.
MULLER:	That's right. In case it was jettisoned or the ship was sunk, the bullion cargo was carried on deck and was fitted with a capsule, which, after two weeks' delay, would automatically detach and float to the surface. There it would send off a coded radio-signal, enabling its position to be determined by two pick-up points on the French coast. It would then emit a green marker-dye at regular intervals.
STOLLEN:	And that's why we are here; to get it back. (*Reflectively*) I wonder if the Fuhrer has been told.
SCHLANGE:	(*turning from the periscope*) If I thought he had not, I would make it my business to see that he was informed
STOLLEN:	Snake, will you never learn? If you open your mouth, I can guarantee that within twenty-four hours you will be on your way to the Eastern Front, where you will have more to think about than your beloved Fuhrer. (*Decisively*) I am going to surface

	and break radio silence. Schmidt!
SCHMIDT:	(*from cubicle*) Kapitan.
STOLLEN:	Take her up.
SCHMIDT:	Ay, ay, sir.
STOLLEN:	Let me have a look. (*He takes the periscope and swings it around.*) Right, we'll---

RADIO OFFICER: (*on intercom*) Message coming through, Kapitan.

STOLLEN leaves the periscope [which SCHLANGE takes] then picks up the telephone.

STOLLEN: (*into telephone*) Put it on.

SHRILL VOICE: Operation Drop-in Command Ship here. U999, where are you? This is the third time we have broken radio silence. Your orders were to meet us here one hour ago. U999, I repeat, where are you, and can you hear me?

STOLLEN: (*into telephone*) I hear you. I am at the designated meeting-point.

COMMAND SHIP: Where is that?

STOLLEN: (*hesitating*) Forty-five, fifty-one north, five-eighteen west.

COMMAND SHIP: That is our position; the correct position. We have found the time-capsule and taken it on board. But we cannot see you. Can you see us?

STOLLEN: No, nothing but empty sea. I am afraid we are at the wrong position. Our instruments must be faulty.

COMMAND SHIP: We can't risk getting a radio fix on your position. Besides, the operation is due to begin. U999 was to provide underwater cover, but we have plenty of surface ships. We have four destroyers and six E-boats, and squadrons of Messerschmitt 109's and Focke-Wulf 190's in relays are giving continuous air cover. If any Allied ship or aeroplane stumbles upon us, they won't live long enough to regret it. Our diving-crew is on deck now, preparing to dive. With luck we'll be sailing back to Germany by this afternoon. With the gold!

STOLLEN: Sir, we will do everything possible to establish our true position, then we will join you.

SCHLANGE: (*excitedly*) Kapitan, the sun has come out! (*The backdrop grows lighter.*)

STOLLEN: (*to MULLER*) Get up top with Schmidt and take a reading with the sextant.

MULLER: Ay, sir. (*He goes into the cubicle*). Come on Schmidt, we're going on deck.

SCHMIDT, followed by MULLER, emerges from the cubicle and they ascend the periscope ladder. The lights fade.
Pause.
The stage lights come on again. STOLLEN, MULLER, SCHLANGE and SCHMIDT are standing at centre-stage. SCHLANGE is poring over a chart, and the others are staring at him.

STOLLEN: Are you sure?

SCHLANGE: Certain, Kapitan. We are approximately twelve miles due south of the meeting-point.

STOLLEN examines the chart; holds it under a light; examines it carefully, then murmurs to himself.

STOLLEN: You're right. (*He steps back from the chart.*)

STOLLEN: Start the engines. Schmidt; set a course due north.

SCHMIDT enters the cubicle, and SCHLANGE and MULLER move towards the controls.

SCHMIDT: (*agitatedly*) Kapitan, the course has changed!

STOLLEN: What? The ship must have turned while we were on deck.

SCHMIDT: No, Kapitan. There is no wind, and the sea is dead calm. The compass reading has changed by five degrees.

STOLLEN: It must be the current.

SCHLANGE: (*alarmed*) Kapitan, there has not been the slightest current for twenty-four hours.

STOLLEN: No time to argue now. Set the course. (To *MULLER and SCHLANGE*) Get the diesels started!

The diesels roar into life, then SCHLANGE goes to the periscope.

STOLLEN: (*picking up the telephone*) Radio Operator. (*Pause.*) Contact the Command Ship. (*Pause.*) Command Ship; we are twelve miles due south of you and are proceeding north at seventeen knots.

COMMAND SHIP: (*from intercom*) Hurry up, or we will be gone before you get here.

STOLLEN: (*laughing*) Keeping all the gold for yourself. Typical dry-feet sailors. You can buy the drinks for that when we all get back to Cuxhaven.

COMMAND SHIP: I am on the bridge. Our recovery team has just gone into the bathyscaphe, which will be lowered to the wreck. Our escort fleet is circling warily, and overhead the Messerschmitts are on the lookout. Ach, what is everyone looking at and pointing to? Yes, now I see. Half-a-dozen fighter planes are approaching, no doubt reinforcements from shore--- (*The harsh note of a klaxon sounds over the intercom.*) They look strange. Can they be our new wonder-jets? (*Enthusiastically*) And there is another wave coming in behind them. They are certainly fast. Himmel, they are attacking our planes! They are British Seafires. (*Gunfire sounds.*) Our ships are answering with everything we have got; cannon; pom-poms; machine-guns. Yes, they have hit one. He is going down in flames. Wunderbar! I see it clearly now. Mein Gott, it is one of ours! (*Panicking*) Now a third wave is approaching; torpedo-carrying Fairey Swordfish---

STOLLEN: (*urgently*) Permission to break off, sir. (*He dials rapidly on the telephone.*) Chief Engineer; can you get anything more out of the engines...? Yes, I know they're going full-out. Could you hook in the electric motors...? Impossible. Well, you know best. Think, man; is there nothing…? Lighten ship? Can you pump out ballast? (*Pause.*) Tanks are empty. We can't jettison fuel or ammunition. Food and drinking-water. They would be negligible, and it's too risky to send men on deck at high speed. What? You can uncouple the speed governors?

Well, do it, man. What? You would have to stop the engines for half-an-hour? That's no use. (*Groans.*) Thanks, Chief. Keep at it. (*He redials.*) Radio Officer, get me the Command Ship.

Pause. A roar of gunfire is heard on the intercom.

COMMAND SHIP: (*desperately*) A destroyer has been torpedoed, and two more of our fighters are down. Ach Gott, now a battleship is coming into view, flanked by a cruiser and destroyer escort. (*Booming is heard, and, on the backdrop, faint flashes are seen distantly on the horizon. There are thunderous bangs, and brighter flashes on the backdrop.*) We have been hit by a shell from the Duke of Cornwall. (*The klaxon sounds again. Shrieking*) The bathyscaphe has disintegrated, and our Commander is dead. It is Abandon Ship! (*There is a much louder bang, and a bright flash on the backdrop, then silence.*)

STOLLEN: (*into telephone*) Command Ship, can you hear me. Repeat, can you hear me? (*He replaces SCHLANGE at the periscope, then peers intently. There is no sound, but, on the backdrop, the flashes intensify. MULLER and SCHLANGE watch with grim faces.*)

Act 4, Scene 2

The stage is dark. MULLER is sitting at his radio in his cabin, and, at centre-stage, CARSTAIRS is at his radio in London.

MULLER: They fell for the oldest trick in the book; a small bag of ball-bearings hanging below the magnetic compass. That was all it took to produce a false indication. I managed to retrieve the bag when I went into the cubicle. The Chief Engineer and Electrical Officer have examined the compass and have found everything in order. So the whole thing remains a mystery. To them, at any rate.

CARSTAIRS: At our end too it was copy-book stuff. After Caramba took the gold from you last month, we dropped the time-capsule and took off with the gold. Then, with the odd careless word and a few false documents and clues, we convinced the German agents that the Caramba, the bullion, and the time-capsule were at the bottom of the Bay of Biscay. At its due time the time-capsule activated. The rest was easy. Winston himself approved the plan, the objective of which was to deal a pulverising blow to the enemy's morale and to weaken his naval strength prior to the invasion. It went like a dream.

MULLER: Were there any losses on our side?

CARSTAIRS: We lost two Swordfish and two Seafires, but the crews were rescued.

MULLER: Thank God. What about Gerry?

CARSTAIRS: Heavy losses. We knocked out every ship and aeroplane. What survivors we managed to pick up are on their way back to the UK.

MULLER: Poor devils.

CARSTAIRS: Yes, poor devils. (*Pause.*) Look, Lieutenant, you've been on that tub for a long time. And it seems to me that, understandably, things have got to you. I am going to ask O to pull you out for a well-earned holiday, then give you a desk job for a while.

MULLER: Not a chance. You know I've been more than useful here, and I am still hoping to get transferred to Naval Intelligence in Berlin. You've far too much to lose by taking me out now. (*Long pause.*) It's just; you spend months, years even, with people and you start getting attached to them; even wretches like Snake. And you develop compassion…

CARSTAIRS: I'll check with O anyway. (*Sternly*) Don't get too compassionate. I don't want to see you hanged as a traitor.

MULLER: You won't.

Act 5, Scene 1

Christmas Eve 1944. The control-room of U 999 in the North Atlantic. The lights come on gradually. The oil-haze is still present in the glaring half-light, and the hum of the propulsion motors is continuous.
The room is decorated with red, white, and black bunting. Near the centre of the room there is a Christmas-tree, on the top of which SCHLANGE is placing a swastika. He steps back to consider the effect, then straightens the flag a little. STOLLEN is at the periscope, with SCHMIDT, unseen, in the control-cubicle. The strains of a choir singing in German, Heilige Nacht (Holy Night), are heard for roughly half-a-minute.

SCHLANGE:	(*turning to STOLLEN*) Christmas. You know, my sister has been writing to my parents from Jersey, asking for food-parcels. I cannot understand it; there is no shortage of food in Germany. (*STOLLEN looks at him and raises his eyebrows, but makes no comment.*)
SCHLANGE:	Of course, I have just realised (*smiles*) she is a sentimental fool, bless her. It will be for the workers in the camp.
STOLLEN:	She is SS, Isn't she?
SCHLANGE:	Of course.
STOLLEN:	Hmm…
SCHLANGE:	(*sentimentally*) I wonder what my parents are doing back in Mecklenburg-Vorpommern.
STOLLEN:	(*grumpily*) Cowering in a bomb-shelter, I would imagine.
SCHLANGE:	(*angrily*) Kapitan; that is defeatist talk. You could be shot on the quayside at Cuxhaven for that.
STOLLEN:	They can shoot me on the backside if they want.
SCHLANGE:	(*reacting and reverting to a strong stage-German accent*) Vell, at least it vood stop your talking out of it.
STOLLEN:	One more death; what does it matter?
SCHLANGE:	(*zealously*) We shall win. Our Fuhrer has said, it is the fate of the hordes of Asia to perish before the gates of Europe's capitals.
STOLLEN:	(*pointing*) This is the last Christmas you'll see under that flag. (*Continuing*) Another ten minutes to dusk. It gets dark abruptly in the Tropics.
SCHLANGE:	(*gazing at him curiously*) Kapitan, we are in the North-Atlantic!
STOLLEN:	(*pointing*) Give me that. (*SCHLANGE hands him a map, which he studies intently; he then turns it upside-down.*) Five hundred curses; no wonder I was bottom of my year in map-reading
SCHLANGE:	(*mystified*) Don't you mean, "One thousand curses"?
STOLLEN:	No, the situation is not that serious. I had better take a look through the periscope, and, if all is well, we will surface and give the crew a chance to get a breath of fresh air. Thanks to this radar it is not safe to be on the surface at night even, but at least they won't be able to see us so easily.
SCHLANGE:	(*earnestly*) Kapitan, you know I would do anything for my Fuhrer; fight on the Eastern Front if it were required; anything.
STOLLEN:	I am sure.
SCHLANGE:	When they transferred me to U-boat Command, I was very

disappointed, since I believed I could serve the Fatherland better by unmasking spies or by running a spy-ring in Britain. However, as time passed, I came to believe that it was all for the best. I was part of a master-plan which would be revealed to me. I feel now that the time is approaching when my fulfilling role will be made clear.

STOLLEN: (*thoughtfully*) Another year almost gone, and we have not seen any real action since that nightmare with the gold-bullion (*pauses.*) we were lucky not to be shot for that.

SCHLANGE: It was mechanical failure, Kapitan. No-one could be blamed for that. I share your feelings of guilt, though.

STOLLEN: (*nodding in agreement*) It's uncanny; it seems that now, whenever there is action, we are somewhere-else. I rack my wits, but can come up with no explanation.

SCHLANGE: Kapitan, could we have a spy on-board?

STOLLEN: If there were, I would have expected you, with your talent for that sort of thing, to have flushed him out before now. But how could he get a report off the ship? There's only the radio-operator, and we all keep close checks on him.

SCHLANGE: (*thoughtfully*) Or he could have a secret radio. (*Eyes narrowing*) Or maybe someone-else has a radio.

STOLLEN: There are only five of us, you, me, Leutnant Muller, Schmidt and the radio-operator, with any significant knowledge. Who can it be?

The door of LEUTNANT MULLER's cabin opens and the Leutnant enters. Both men turn to stare at him.

MULLER: Reporting for watch, Kapitan.

STOLLEN: Leutnant, we think there may be a spy on board.

MULLER: I know.

STOLLEN and SCHLANGE: (*together*) You know!

STOLLEN: How do you know?

MULLER: I am the Security Officer.

SCHLANGE: Well, who is it?

MULLER: I suspect it could be the ship's cat.

STOLLEN: (*exchanging an incredulous glance with SCHLANGE*) The ship's cat! That is absolutely ridiculous. He jumped ship two hours before you arrived, and was last seen stowing away on a herring-drifter on the Frisian coast.

MULLER: (*calmly*) I had my suspicions. I had seen a report that two cats had started scrounging from the cookhouse at Cuxhaven.

SCHLANGE: I heard about that. They had name-tags; Tom and Jerry.

MULLER: Two small parachutes were found buried nearby.

SCHLANGE: I remember that too. Security spent months hunting for two dwarfs, but never found them.

MULLER: Jerry is now the official mouser to the Director of Operations. I think Tom took off because he knew I was on his tail.

SCHLANGE: (*slapping his thigh and laughing uproariously*) Leutnant, he is a Manx cat. (*Laughs.*) Oh, that's good; you were on his tail.

MULLER: I fear he crept back on board and is in hiding.

STOLLEN: Have you any evidence for that?

MULLER:	Have you read the cook's stocktaking reports lately?
STOLLEN:	I have. Regular pilfering of fish; nothing-else except a small tin of cream.
MULLER:	That is Tom, I fear.
STOLLEN:	But how could a cat spy?
MULLER:	The Yanks have done a lot of work lately on the increasing of animal intelligence. Their stated aim is to put a donkey in the White House. I believe Tom and Jerry are British agents. Tell me, did Tom have a collar?
SCHLANGE:	Yes, a very elaborate affair with a number of sparkling, jewelled studs around it: rubies, emeralds, and amethysts. Sometimes they seemed to glow with inner fires.
MULLER:	His radio.
STOLLEN:	But how could he use it? He couldn't talk--or could he?
MULLER:	I believe he miaowed his reports in Morse-code.
SCHLANGE:	But, as a Manx cat, he probably couldn't understand English.
MULLER:	I imagine he is tri-lingual. The Manx emblem has three legs. I think Tom has three tongues. In a manner of speaking.
SCHLANGE:	That's very good. (*STOLLEN nods in agreement.*)
SCHLANGE:	(*thoughtfully*) Leutnant, you have a very strange accent.
MULLER:	(*changing to a comical stage-German accent*) Vood you hef me talk in zer vay zat you do? (Reverting to middle-class English accent) Actually, I was educated at the International School in Hamburg, where the staff are all English. That is how I acquired this accent.
SCHLANGE:	Hmm. Kapitan, once more I have the feeling that momentous events are imminent. I have sources in Berlin.
MULLER:	(*needled*) You should have brought them. That last bockwurst the cook dished up was rank.
SCHLANGE:	Not that sort of sauce. Informants, who tell me that our leader is negotiating with the American President.
MULLER:	I know, I know. The President will say, "I am a doughnut".
STOLLEN:	What is this about a doughnut?
MULLER:	(*aside to the audience*) Sorry, I am about twenty years too early. Kennedy will say that in Berlin.
SCHLANGE:	Yes, he is not bothering with Churchill, that evil ironmonger.
MULLER:	Do you mean, "warmonger"?
SCHLANGE:	Whoremonger?
MULLER:	Same thing.
SCHLANGE:	(*dreamily*) Our beloved Fuhrer visited our academy once. (*Poses theatrically.*) I was one of the honour-guard; they were all there; Marschall Goering, Dr Goebbels, Heinrich Himmler; "faithful Heini", and, very discreetly, Eva Braun.
MULLER:	Who is that?
STOLLEN:	(*looking mystified*) Eva Braun. Never heard of her.
SCHLANGE:	(*posturing*) She is the Fuhrer's trusted right-hand (*turns to smirk at the audience.*) and his left, when they are both tired.

All three enjoy the joke.

| STOLLEN: | It must be dark by now. Schmidt, periscope-depth. |
| SCHMIDT: | Jawohl, Kapitan. |

STOLLEN waits by the periscope, while MULLER and SCHLANGE attend to other tasks.

SCHMIDT: Periscope-depth it is, Kapitan.

STOLLEN raises the periscope. The back-drop above the set is pitch-black; several stars wink faintly into life.

STOLLEN: As black as the inside of a coal-miner's--- Take it, Snake.

SCHLANGE looks through the periscope.

SCHLANGE: Might as well be one hundred fathoms down, for all I can see.

STOLLEN: I think I'll take a chance and surface. Keep looking, and you, Muller, have a listen on the hydrophones. (*MULLER sits down and places the hydrophones on his head.*)

MULLER: What about the night-scope?

STOLLEN: Night-scope?

MULLER: Yes, infra-red or light-intensification viewer. (*Puts his hand to his mouth, then half-turns to the audience.*) Oh, God, I keep forgetting; it's only nineteen forty-four.

STOLLEN: I'll see whether or not I can order one when we get back to Cuxhaven. Anything, Snake?

SCHLANGE: Just waves and the odd fish or two, Kapitan.

STOLLEN: Interesting. Have another look, Muller. See if you can identify them. I'm thinking about writing a book on marine wildlife when this is all over.

MULLER: Fortunately, I have extremely good night-vision. (*He looks through the periscope. Some of the stars disappear.*) Yes, I can see something.

STOLLEN: A fish? It could be a little treat for Tom, when we catch him and put him in the ship's gaol. (*Thoughtfully*) I wonder whether the ship's tailor could knock up a little convict's suit for him, striped, of course.

MULLER: No, a ship off the port-quarter.

STOLLEN: Let me see. (*Takes the periscope.*) Not a thing. Are you sure?

MULLER: Very.

STOLLEN: Snake.

SCHLANGE takes a long look through the periscope.

SCHLANGE: (*Slowly*) If anything; it looks even darker.

STOLLEN: Muller.

MULLER: (*peering through the periscope*) It is still there; to port and gradually catching us up.

STOLLEN: What is it?

MULLER: I have no doubt , Kapitan, that we have finally caught up with the Royal Navy battleship, Duke of Cornwall.

STOLLEN and SCHLANGE: (*exchanging glances, together*) What?

STOLLEN: You are sure?

MULLER: One hundred percent. Kapitan.

STOLLEN: You are quite certain?

MULLER: One thousand percent. Kapitan, we haven't much time.

STOLLEN: Let me see. (*He takes the periscope.*) Curses; I might as well have my head up my--- Take it, Snake.

SCHLANGE: (*looking*) Wait a minute; we have moonlight. (*On the backdrop the indistinct image of a large warship appears. Uncertainly*)

	It is certainly a battleship. (*He hesitates.*) If anything, I would say it looks like the Schweinhund.
STOLLEN:	Muller!
MULLER:	Kapitan.
STOLLEN:	Recognition-manual.
MULLER:	Sir. (*He goes to the small cabinet beside the periscope, and takes out a blue, linen-backed book, then leafs rapidly through it. He hands the open book to STOLLEN, who studies it with interest, then passes it to SCHLANGE.*)
STOLLEN:	(*to SCHLANGE*) Well?

SCHLANGE peers closely at the book, then gazes through the periscope. He looks back at the book, then blinks and peers at length through the periscope.

SCHLANGE:	(*turning to STOLLEN*) I cannot understand it. It is definitely the Duke of Cornwall. (*He places his hand behind his head in a gesture of puzzlement.*) And yet; it looks so different to what I remember.
STOLLEN:	Muller?
MULLER:	I say it is The Duke of Cornwall.
STOLLEN:	(*taking the book from SCHLANGE, then examining it*) We have a score to settle with that ship. Action stations!

SCHLANGE presses a button; the klaxon screeches, and there are bangs and the sound of running feet.

STOLLEN:	Muller; take the periscope. You have cats' eyes. (*MULLER takes the periscope.*) Estimated range and speed of target.

SCHLANGE goes to the torpedo-launcher.

MULLER:	Five hundred yards and twelve knots.
SCHLANGE:	Why didn't you say, "metres"?
STOLLEN:	We've been into all that before. Schmidt; full speed ahead.
SCHMIDT:	Full speed ahead it is, Kapitan.
STOLLEN:	Pick your time, Muller. Fire three torpedoes; spaced.
MULLER:	Ay, ay, sir. Target almost in-line. (*He pauses.*) Fire one.

SCHLANGE pulls the firing-lever.

STOLLEN:	(*begins to count slowly.*) One--two---
MULLER:	Fire two. (*SCHLANGE pulls the firing-lever.*) Fire three.

SCHLANGE pulls the firing-lever.

STOLLEN:	--eleven--twelve---

There is a thunderous detonation and the control-room shakes. Simultaneously there is a vivid flash near the stem of the target ship.

MULLER:	Hit forward.
STOLLEN:	--seventeen---(*Another detonation and a flash amidships.*)
MULLER:	Hit 'midships.
STOLLEN:	--twenty-two. (*Another detonation and a flash near the stern.*)
MULLER:	Hit aft.
STOLLEN:	Target damage report.
MULLER:	Three fires burning. (*On the backdrop the ship is well-alight.*)
STOLLEN:	Let me see. (*Peers.*) Prepare for counter-attack. Make ready to dive.
SCHMIDT:	Ay, ay, Kapitan.
STOLLEN:	Here, Muller. Take it, and keep on reporting.
MULLER:	(*solemnly*) Kapitan, the great ship is sinking. (*The sinking is

44

depicted on the backdrop.) Oh God, this is awful. She is rolling to port, so she is unable to bring any of her weapons to bear on us. We are very fortunate.

Now the crew are launching life-boats. Hurry up, she is going down fast. Yes, every boat is launched. No, a few of the crew are jumping off. They are swimming away from their ship. Hurry up!

STOLLEN: Surface!

SCHLANGE and SCHMIDT: Ay, ay, Kapitan.

STOLLEN: Snake, make ready with the guns and searchlight.

SCHLANGE: (*enthusiastically*) Should I machine-gun them in the water, Kapitan?

STOLLEN: (*furiously*) The only one to be machine-gunned will be you, after I throw you in.

MULLER: Survivors approaching; about half-a-dozen of them.

STOLLEN: (*shouting*) Pick up survivors.

The set, control-room and burning ship, which is rapidly disappearing beneath the waves, slowly darkens.

Act 5, Scene 2

The control-room; half an hour later. STOLLEN is studying a gauge. He taps it. MULLER is sitting, staring at a bulkhead. He is preoccupied and pensive. SCHLANGE enters from the forward door.

SCHLANGE: *(excitedly)* Kapitan, they are still insisting that they are Germans; all six of them. I told the one who claims to be the Kapitan, that I will shoot him if he says it once more.

STOLLEN: *(jumping in alarm)* No need for that, Snake.

SCHLANGE: He told me I was a typical Nazi. I think he was trying to flatter me. They do speak excellent German, though. They are clearly extremely well-trained.

STOLLEN: Well, let's see how long they keep up this nonsense. What do you think, Muller? *(MULLER does not hear him.)* Leutnant, what do you think?

MULLER: *(whipping around in alarm, stammering)* What?

STOLLEN: What do you think?

MULLER: *(blankly)* About what?

STOLLEN: *(staring in puzzlement)* Their claiming to be German.

MULLER: *(recovering his poise with difficulty)* A typical, sly, English trick. That's what it was. It was unmistakeably the Duke of Cornwall. I just hope everyone survives. As for that ridiculous pretence at being Germans; they are planning to seize our ship if we give them half a chance.

STOLLEN: *(looking at him closely)* Are you all right? You look very pale.

MULLER: I'm all right.

A telephone rings and STOLLEN picks it up.

STOLLEN: Kapitan here.

RADIO OPERATOR: Radio Operator reporting. Kapitan, I have just picked up a signal from a lifeboat of the ship we sank. They said it happened so quickly that the ship had no time to get off a signal.

STOLLEN: Yes?

RADIO OPERATOR: Kapitan, they were signalling Berlin. They claim they are from the Schweinhund.

STOLLEN: *(slowly)* But why would the English claim that?

RADIO OPERATOR: Kapitan, I fear we have sunk the Schweinhund.

STOLLEN: Are you sure?

RADIO OPERATOR: The message was clear as a bell, Kapitan. Since recording equipment will not be invented for a year or two yet, I typed it; every word.

STOLLEN: *(putting the telephone down)* I cannot understand it. The book was so clear. *(Stiffening)* Snake, the recognition-manual!

SCHLANGE goes to the small locker beside the periscope, and takes out the blue manual, then hands it to STOLLEN.

STOLLEN: *(leafing rapidly through the manual)* Dainty, Daring, Diana, Dido, Dildo, Dorsetshire. *(He pauses, and stands as though thunderstruck, then hands the book to SCHLANGE, who studies the open pages.)*

SCHLANGE: *(disbelievingly)* Duke of Cornwall--- *(He scrabbles through*

	the pages.) Scharnhorst, Schickelgruber, Schinkenwurst. (*Still disbelieving*) Schweinhund? Kapitan, we have sunk the Schweinhund!
STOLLEN:	How can this be? Let me see it. (*He takes the manual and studies it closely*) What has happened? This is not possible. All three of us looked at the silhouettes. We couldn't all be wrong. Have we been hypnotised, or were we all hallucinating?
SCHLANGE:	Drugged?
STOLLEN:	Our last battleship. And we sank it. (*To SCHLANGE*) Come on; we'll have a good look at that report, and have another word with the prisoners. (*To MULLER*) Take command here until I come back. And don't fire at anything (pauses.) especially if it's British.

Act 5, Scene 3

Half an hour later. MULLER is sitting at the radio in his cabin. He presses a key. The first few bars of the music for the song "Ay--ay--ay--ay--ay--I like you vairee much" are heard. CARSTAIRS' head and shoulders appear inset. He presses a key, there is a crackle of static, then the music for "Indian Love Call" is heard briefly.

MULLER:	Agent U here.
CARSTAIRS:	Agent I here.
MULLER:	I've really done it this time.
CARSTAIRS:	What?
MULLER:	Sunk the Schweinhund.
CARSTAIRS:	What?
MULLER:	I've sunk the Schweinhund.
CARSTAIRS:	*(gasping)* Whew! *(He sits back, quite at a loss for words. He gasps again.)* That's unbelievable. Good Lord; it's marvellous. It will take the load off the Home Fleet, our convoy escorts and off Coastal Command. How did you manage it?
MULLER:	It was there, and I convinced them it was the Duke of Cornwall. I substituted that dummy recognition-manual which the lab had prepared, with the silhouettes for the two ships swapped around, for the real one. Then after the sinking, I changed them around again. They still can't understand what has happened. I'm afraid it's all up, though.
CARSTAIRS:	I can see that life will be extremely unpleasant for all of you.
MULLER:	We picked up Schweinhund's captain and several crew members, and our radio-operator picked up a message from one of their lifeboats. Stollen has radioed Berlin and told them what has happened. We are heading back to Cuxhaven at top speed. We will, of course, all be executed, and, apart from that, it can't be long before Stollen or Schlange realises that the spy can only be me.
CARSTAIRS:	You didn't have to sacrifice yourself, you know.
MULLER:	What would you have done?
CARSTAIRS:	*(pausing, then slowly)* I like to think I would have had the courage to do the same.
MULLER:	I wonder how many casualties there were. I saw a lot of boats being launched.
CARSTAIRS:	Lieutenant, I have warned you not to get sentimental. You knew when you volunteered that you would be involved in extremely nasty affairs.
MULLER:	*(quietly)* I know. My cyanide capsule is in place. Five seconds and it will all be over.
CARSTAIRS:	Not so hasty; there's more at stake than your life, important as it is. You see, there are immense things afoot, which will soon come to a head---
MULLER:	*(laughs.)* Things afoot, coming to a head.
CARSTAIRS:	Please, Lieutenant; be serious. There are plans which I am not at liberty to disclose at present. You are vitally needed on U999. That is why O wouldn't pull you out earlier this year,

	when I wanted to. We've got to do something.
MULLER:	Take your time, I'm not going anywhere.
CARSTAIRS:	(*slowly*) I need time to think (*pauses.*) yes, there's just a chance. I know your approximate position; you had better give me the precise coordinates. O is just next door. I'm going now to see him. We've got to act fast. Stay tuned in.

The set slowly darkens.

Act 5, Scene 4

The following day. STOLLEN, MULLER and SCHLANGE are in the control-room. All three look worried. The oil-haze is visible in the harsh light; the diesels rattle continuously. MULLER is checking gauges, and SCHLANGE is peering through the periscope. STOLLEN paces across the control-room and back.

STOLLEN:	(*half to himself*) Full-speed, they ordered., so we have to stay on the surface. It will be dark in four hours; we will be safer then. (*Moodily*) It seems we were fated to sink the Schweinhund. I will swing for it.
MULLER:	(*sympathetically*) It wasn't just your mistake, Kapitan.
STOLLEN:	I am the Kapitan; I take the blame, and, when we are charged, I will point out that we would have sunk the Schweinhund last year, but for you.
SCHLANGE:	(*turning from the periscope*) All three of us will get it. I am the First Officer, and I made the same mistake as you, although to me the profile did not look like that of the Duke of Cornwall. That book remains a mystery.
STOLLEN:	The lighting is terrible. (*Doubtfully*) That might be the explanation.
SCHLANGE:	(*scornfully*) I will not use that as my excuse.
STOLLEN:	Tell them you thought it was the Schweinhund.
SCHLANGE:	Nor that. Whatever the reason; I will not seek to blame others for my stupidity.

STOLLEN and MULLER stare at him in surprise.

SCHLANGE:	Oh, I know what you think of me. I am not called Snake for nothing. I have lied, cheated and betrayed for the Reich, and I will not hesitate to do so in future, because I know it is right. But I will not lie just to save my own skin.
STOLLEN:	Surely, you can serve the Reich better with your skin intact.
SCHLANGE:	(*turning away*) The Reich has no need of cowards. (*He peers through the periscope.*) There is a ship coming.

The silhouette, very small, of a cargo-ship, appears on the left of the backdrop. MULLER starts, but STOLLEN remains pre-occupied.

STOLLEN:	They say they hang people on meat-hooks these days, and film their death-agonies. (*Sighs.*) A film-star at last. Not much chance of repeat roles, though.
SCHLANGE:	Kapitan, there is a ship coming.
STOLLEN:	(*still pensive*) I'll take a look. (*He takes the periscope.*) Yes, I see it, abaft and coming up fast.

The ship is now larger and is progressing across the backdrop.

STOLLEN:	Sound Action Stations.

SCHLANGE presses a button and the klaxon screeches; there are bangs and the sound of running feet. SCHLANGE goes to the torpedo-launcher.

STOLLEN:	Down to periscope depth..
SCHMIDT:	Jawohl, Kapitan.
STOLLEN:	Take a look, Muller. (*MULLER takes the periscope.*) What do you think?
MULLER:	Looks like a Bibby-line ship to me, sir. Unmistakeably, I would say.

STOLLEN:	Snake!
SCHLANGE:	(*leaving the torpedo-launcher and taking the periscope*) I agree with the Leutnant. A Bibby-liner of thirty-thousand tons, one of four built by Swan-Hunter, with double-reduction geared Parsons turbines supplied by the Wallsend Slipway, and forced-draught, oil-fired Cochran water-tube boilers. Originally built for the frozen meat trade and very fast; since converted to an ammunition and troop-carrier, with two Vickers six-inch guns forward and after. Far superior to anything we Germans ever produced. (*He stands back and blinks.*) Himmel, did I say that? I must say, she looks very high out of the water.
STOLLEN:	I'll take it. (*SCHLANGE returns to the torpedo-launcher.*)
STOLLEN:	(*peering through the periscope*) My first thought was a Bibby-line ship. We are all agreed on that. There is no-one at the guns, and no-one running about. No change of speed or direction. Not a sign of activity. Either they have not seen us or they are playing a clever game and are preparing to ram us. I estimate about one minute to target range.
MULLER:	(*urgently*) Kapitan, we are all agreed. We must attack.

On the backdrop the ship is now large and close.

SCHLANGE:	Kapitan, please.
STOLLEN:	(*calmly*) Prepare to fire.
SCHLANGE:	Ready to fire, Kapitan.
STOLLEN:	Wait for it.... Fire one. (*SCHLANGE pulls the firing-lever, and STOLLEN begins to count slowly.*) One...two--fire two...fire three...nine...ten...eleven...twelve.

There are three thunderous detonations, spaced out, accompanied by vivid flashes on the backdrop, and the control-room shakes, knocking the Christmas-tree askew.

STOLLEN:	Perfect; text-book stuff. Mein Gott, she goes down fast. (*On the backdrop, the ship rapidly sinks.*) Take us up, Schmidt.
SCHMIDT:	Surface it is, Kapitan.
MULLER:	Any sign of boats being launched, Kapitan?
STOLLEN:	Not a sign of anything.
MULLER:	Thank God.

STOLLEN and SCHLANGE turn with puzzled looks. STOLLEN looks horrified, while SCHLANGE suddenly slaps his thigh and laughs with glee.

STOLLEN:	Leutnant?
MULLER:	(*hastily*) I mean, for giving us such an easy target.
STOLLEN:	Hmm....Well, we'll have a good sweep as soon as we get the hatch open, but I fear we won't find any survivors. It's as though the ship never existed.

Act 5, Scene 5

Half-an-hour later. The control-room of U999. STOLLEN is sitting by the periscope; MULLER is reading a technical manual, and SCHLANGE is at the Christmas-tree, straightening the swastika.

SCHLANGE:　　What a Christmas present; to sink such a target. The Fuhrer's stars were surely shining on us today. (*Smiles expansively.*) Maybe they will give us a medal before they shoot us.

STOLLEN:　　(*looking up*) Something funny about the whole business. That ship just sailed up; didn't spot us; didn't launch any life-boats; just sank like a stone.

MULLER:　　Just think of all the tanks and guns and ammunition at the bottom of the Atlantic.

STOLLEN:　　(*brightening*) Better there than in Germany.

RADIO OPERATOR'S VOICE: (*from intercom*) Kapitan, important bulletin coming through in one minute.

STOLLEN:　　For general information?

RADIO OPERATOR: Ja, Kapitan.

STOLLEN:　　Put me on the loudspeaker.

RADIO OPERATOR: Kapitan.

STOLLEN:　　Achtung all hands. Prepare for an important bulletin,

After a pause, there is a buzz, gradually diminishing, from the loudspeaker. A call-signal, the first few bars of Deutschland uber Alles, sounds twice.

HIGH-PITCHED EXCITED VOICE: Hier ist Berliner Rundfunk.

A rousing, Prussian march is heard. STOLLEN, MULLER and SCHLANGE gaze at each other expectantly. The music stops.

STOLLEN:　　Now we are for it. The trio exchange glances.

EXCITED VOICE: Our glorious forces in the North Atlantic have achieved yet another fantastic victory. U999 has within the hour torpedoed and sunk a large British ammunition-carrier, carrying vital supplies to the hard-pressed Allies, who are already reeling under the relentless onslaught of the Fuhrer's brilliantly conceived Ardennes Offensive.

Guy Fawkes' Day has come a little late for the Tommies, and it is one they won't be celebrating. Reports speak of a blazing inferno, with exploding shells and bombs sending hundreds of fiery streamers high into the clouds as tanks, guns and aeroplanes descend to, as Tommy would say, Davy Jones's Locker.

It is confidently anticipated that this crushing defeat of the enemies of the Reich will bring the end of the war significantly closer. (*Pause.*) Heil Hitler!

The three officers raise their hands very half-heartedly in the Nazi salute.

ALL THREE:　　(*weakly*) Heil Hitler! (*They exchange dumbfounded looks.*)

MULLER:　　Well…

SCHLANGE:　　(*lacking conviction*) It must be part of Dr Goebbels' grand, propaganda strategy to devastate the morale of the enemy.

STOLLEN:　　(*slowly*) Not a mention of the loss of the Schweinhund. They keep that quiet, then fabricate that gross lie about the sinking of the liner. The way it went down, it was just as though it was

	a ghost ship, or at least an empty ship; not a sign of life on it.
SCHLANGE:	I am sure it is all part of our wise Fuhrer's master-plan.
STOLLEN:	(*quietly*) Shut up, Snake.

Act 6, Scene 1

January 1945. An office in Naval Intelligence, London. To the right of the set there is a table at which is seated COMMANDER MORRISON, "O", facing left. At his right is CAPTAIN CARSTAIRS, "I". Both are in naval uniform. Facing them at the far left, at a desk, is a secretary, MISS MILLBANK. She is attractive, with fair, permed hair, and has horn-rimmed spectacles. She is dressed somewhat dowdily, in a rather thickly knitted patterned cardigan, a grey skirt, and plain shoes. On her desk there are a typists' pad and a pencil, which she picks up. At the front of stage left (behind MISS MILLBANK) there is a door to the corridor. MORRISON's telephone rings. He picks it up.

MORRISON:	O. (*Listens, then heartily*) Come on up. (*To MISS MILLBANK*) How are you, Miss Marchbank?
MISS MILLBANK:	It is Millbank, Commander.
MORRISON:	(*clearly taken aback*) Are you sure?
MISS MILLBANK:	Positive.
MORRISON:	(*bluffly*) Of course. So how are things in Broadstairs?
MISS MILLBANK:	I can check for you, Commander.
MORRISON:	Don't you live there?
MISS MILLBANK:	I live in Edgware.

MORRISON leans back, digesting the information. The doorbell sounds.

MORRISON:	(*to MISS MILLBANK, genially*) Tell U to come in.
MISS MILLBANK:	(*puzzled*) I?
MORRISON:	(*pointing at CARSTAIRS*) No, I is already here. Tel U to come in.
MISS MILLBANK:	Commander, as you would say, I is already here.
MORRISON:	(*clearly perplexed*) I just said, "I is here".
MISS MILLBANK:	(*laughing*) Commander, to use your way of speech, I know that you is here.
MORRISON:	(*in turn laughing*) That is the whole point; U is not here.
CARSTAIRS:	(*hastily*) Let me explain: I am I.
MISS MILLBANK:	That is obvious. We are all I.
MORRISON:	(*good-humouredly*) Well, at least we are all agreed on that. (*Leaning forward, emphatically*) But it is U I want.
MISS MILLBANK:	Oh! (*She bridles, clearly embarrassed but pleased at the interest shown in her, sets the writing pad down, then unconsciously draws the two halves of her cardigan together and pats the back of her hair.*)
MORRISON:	(*patiently*) No, not you, U.
MISS MILLBANK:	(*puzzled once more*) Ah!
MORRISON:	No, R is on duty in Berlin. (*He pauses.*) It's just occurred to me; have you been cleared by Security?
MISS MILLBANK:	No, actually, I'm only a temp.
MORRISON:	No matter. (*He winks at CARSTAIRS.*) No secrets here, what?
CARSTAIRS:	(*laughing sycophantically*) Oh, rather, sir.
MORRISON:	Let's start all over again. (*He breaks off.*) I hope you're taking all this down. I want U in here.
MISS MILLBANK:	Eh?
MORRISON:	Don't bring A into it. He is in Moscow. U.
MISS MILLBANK:	Commander, we have been into all that. I am here; you are

here. We are all here.

CARSTAIRS: Sir, may I interrupt? (*To MISS MILLBANK*) I am I (*points.*) he is O. You are Miss Ewbank---

MISS MILLBANK: Millbank!

CARSTAIRS: Quite, but U is outside.

MISS MILLBANK: (*infuriated*) Are you blind? I am here.

CARSTAIRS: (*smiling*) Try again. (*Pointing to himself*) I. (*Pointing to the door*) U.

MISS MILLBANK, confused, stands up and prepares to leave.

CARSTAIRS: No; sit down. (*Pointing to himself*) I.

MISS MILLBANK: Oh.

CARSTAIRS: Yes, and we both want U.

MISS MILLBANK: (*tossing her head back*) Form a queue.

CARSTAIRS: (*helpfully*) U is outside.

MISS MILLBANK: (*talking to the door*) Is you out there?

MILLER: (*offstage*) I certainly is.

MORRISON: (*a little exasperated*) Ewbank, Lloyd's Bank, organ-bank, Dogger Bank--what the hell. U, get in here; fast.

The door opens and LIEUTENANT MILLER strides in. He is in British naval uniform and is wearing his peaked cap.

MILLER: (*to MISS MILLBANK, smiling*) I am U. (*Pointing to CARSTAIRS*) He is I.

MISS MILLBANK: (*mystified*) Oh!.

MILLER: (*pointing to MORRISON*) That's right.

MORRISON: (*holding out both arms to include CARSTAIRS and MILLER*) We three!

MISS MILLBANK: (*shrugging, muttering, casting her eyes upwards*) Just a set of twerps, maybe.

MORRISON: (*rising to shake MILLER's hand*) 'Morning, U.

MILLER: 'Morning, O. 'Morning, I.

CARSTAIRS: 'Morning, U.

MORRISON: (*beaming*) This is Miss Blood-bank. (*Triumphantly*) I got it right this time.

MILLER and MISS MILLBANK: (*together*) Good morning.

MORRISON: We make a damned good team. I--O--U! (*Laughs.*) Lend us a tenner!

CARSTAIRS: (*smiling obsequiously*) Oh, very good, Commander.

MISS MILLBANK: (*turning to grimace at the audience*) I'm going to have a lot of fun with this lot.

MILLER: (*taking a seat at the table*) That was a brilliant ruse, sir.

MISS MILLBANK begins to take notes.

MORRISON: Don't thank me; it was Captain Carstairs' idea.

MILLER: It saved me from torture and the firing-squad, or a cyanide capsule at best. It was lucky you had that ammunition-ship returning empty, and you managed to get all the crew off before aiming her at U999. It fooled Berlin, apparently, since Stollen, Snake and I are to be awarded a bar to our Iron Crosses, and the crew are all getting extra leave.

CARSTAIRS: What about the Schweinhund sinking?

MILLER: Nothing has been said so far, which is puzzling, since a very full report of the incident was sent to Berlin, and I don't see how our agent there could cover that up.

MORRISON and CARSTAIRS exchange significant glances.

MORRISON: So far, so good, Carstairs.

CARSTAIRS: Let's hope so, sir.

MORRISON: Well done. (*To MILLER*) We got you out alive, and that's the important thing.

MILLER: (*quietly*) Thank you, sir.

MORRISON: Actually, as Carstairs told you, there is something very big afoot, which you will be very much involved in, and that is the reason why we sacrificed a large ship, and, it goes without saying, we could not risk your divulging what you know. And it is also partly the reason why you have been so long on U999 instead of going back to Berlin following your initial six months assignment to gain experience. I can't tell you any more at present.

MILLER: That's interesting, because Snake keeps bleating on about a master-plan he's involved in.

MORRISON: (*sharply to CARSTAIRS*) I wonder how much he knows.

CARSTAIRS: I wonder. He does have contacts in Berlin.

MORRISON: So it's back to Cuxhaven for you, Miller. We'll tell you what we can, when we can. But take care; we don't want to lose you. Any questions, Miss Sperm-bank? (*Eyes twinkling*) We don't want any mistakes with names, do we?

MISS MILLBANK: (*absolutely raging*) You can count on that. I'll type up the minutes.

MORRISON: Right-ho! Just file them under I O U. That's in the drawer marked, Petty Cash.

Act 6, Scene 2

January 1945. An office in the Naval Intelligence bunker in Berlin, dominated, at the rear, by a large colour portrait of Adolf Hitler. At the right of the set ADMIRAL SCHLEIM is sitting at a long table and is facing across the set. There is a chair in front of the table. HAUPTMANN AUTOTREPPEN (CARSTAIRS) is sitting at the end of the table, with his back to the audience. His face is not disclosed to the audience throughout the scene. Both men are in uniform. There is a knock and LEUTNANT SCHLANGE enters from a door at the left.

SCHLANGE: (*turning to the portrait, then clicking his heels and giving the Nazi salute*) Heil Hitler!

SCHLEIM and AUTOTREPPEN: (*saluting but remaining seated*) Heil Hitler!

SCHLEIM: (*motioning SCHLANGE to sit*) You wanted to see me.

SCHLANGE glances at AUTOTREPPEN.

SCHLEIM: (*indicating AUTOTREPPEN*) This is A.

SCHLANGE: Eh?

SCHLEIM: That's right.

AUTOTREPPEN: (*hastily*) Please, Admiral, let us try to avoid any confusion over code-letters. Time is pressing.

SCHLEIM: Of course. Let me explain, Leutnant. We all have code-letters. His (*pointing at AUTOTREPPEN*) is A. Mine is (*hissing like a snake*) Sss.

SCHLANGE: (*laughing*) That should be mine. My friends call me Snake.

SCHLEIM: (*bleakly*) I can see why. Now get on with it.

SCHLANGE: I believe we have a spy in our midst.

SCHLEIM: (*coldly*) Only one? How do you know?

SCHLANGE: I have my sources.

SCHLEIM: Who are?

SCHLANGE: I cannot divulge their names.

SCHLEIM: (*purple-faced and shouting*) What? Do you want me to hand you over to our friends in the Gestapo?

SCHLANGE: (*keeping calm, and looking up at the portrait*) Admiral, my loyalty is only to the Fuhrer and Reich. The first major incident was when U999, on which as you know I am First Officer, encountered a battleship, which Leutnant Muller, our Security Officer, insisted was a Schweinhund-class battleship. I have now ascertained that there was no such ship within three thousand kilometres of our position. That ship was in fact the Duke of Cornwall, and we would have sunk it but for the actions of our Security Officer.

SCHLEIM: I know of no such incident.

SCHLANGE: With respect, sir, that is because I believe a British agent here in Berlin was able to block or falsify the report from U999. The British agent is code-named R.

SCHLEIM and AUTOTREPPEN exchange glances.

SCHLANGE: The next incident occurred when we, that is Kapitan Stollen and I, were duped into handing our cargo of gold to the British, and there followed the disaster of the destruction of the retrieval fleet which had been lured to the scene. Someone on U999 was in constant communication with the British. Finally, by some trick which I still do not understand, we were fooled into sinking our own Schweinhund. We then managed, in very suspicious circumstances, to sink a British ammunition-carrier. I am sure that Leutnant Muller hopes it will save his skin. (*He pauses and draws back on his chair.*) I am certain that Leutnant Muller is the spy.

SCHLEIM does not reply, but stares expressionlessly at SCHLANGE, who in turn stares back neutrally.

SCHLEIM: (*after perhaps half-a-minute*) Well, that is some statement, Leutnant. Quite a confession to make. Let me get it straight. You failed to attack the enemy's prime capital ship. Next you lost a cargo of gold which could be crucial for the survival of the Fatherland, which in turn led to the annihilation of a small fleet. Finally you manage to sink Germany's last battleship. (*He pauses.*) You could end up dangling from a meat-hook, along with others who may be judged in dereliction of duty; for example, Autotreppen--(*CARSTAIRS, who has been listening quietly, jumps in fright.*)--or me. (He lowers his voice, persuasively.) Now, none of us would want that: would we Leutnant?

SCHLANGE: I admit my own guilt, but it is more important to apprehend Leutnant Muller before he commits any more acts of sabotage.

SCHLEIM: Leutnant, your sense of duty does you great credit, but let me enlighten you. Hauptmann Autotreppen and I have just spent two days examining the records of U999. They are quite clear. U999 made contact with an unidentified warship, which engaged you heavily. It was only through the prompt actions of Leutnant Muller and Kapitan Stollen that you survived.

SCHLANGE: Admiral, with the greatest respect, the records have been falsified.

SCHLEIM: (*in a low voice*) Forget it, Leutnant. It is a closed book. As for the loss of the gold and the retrieval fleet; the Fuhrer was furious, but then the Fuhrer is frequently furious. He was impressed with Leutnant Muller's notion of using the green marker-dye, however. He blames the disaster on the actions of the British agent, R.

SCHLANGE: You know of him?

SCHLEIM: Hauptmann Autotreppen will explain.

AUTOTREPPEN: We had long had suspicions about Agent R. I was sent to arrest him but found his office deserted. Someone had tipped him off.

SCHLANGE: So there is still a spy on the loose here in Berlin.

AUTOTREPPEN: It would appear so. I am sure R could have given us lots of useful information, but he was last seen on a sledge drawn by a team of Pyrenean mountain dogs en route for neutral Portugal. A pity.

SCHLANGE: But what about the Schweinhund?

SCHLEIM: (*carefully*) The Fuhrer does not know about the sinking of the Schweinhund.

SCHLANGE: (*looking at the portrait and aghast*) You have not told him!

SCHLEIM:	(*stealthily*) Would you like to tell him, Leutnant?
SCHLANGE:	If it be necessary, yes.
SCHLEIM:	Now listen, Leutnant. Within the hour I can have you transferred to the Eastern Front, where, I can promise you, the only correspondence for you will be in the form of lead from the Russian hordes who at this moment are storming into the Reich.
SCHLANGE:	(*determinedly*) But Leutnant Muller is a spy. And there is something very different about him; something I cannot put my finger on, but I know he is a spy.
SCHLEIM:	(*coldly*) Leutnant Muller is one of the Fuhrer's favourites, and, unless you want to be on the next train east, you will stop airing your views about your fellow-officers and these imaginary happenings. (He speaks in a friendly, conciliatory tone.) Leutnant, the Fuhrer is delighted with the sinking of the Bibby liner, with all the tanks, aeroplanes, lorries and ammunition she was carrying. He is convinced that U999 is a lucky ship; it is in fact our longest-surviving U-boat, and his stars have informed him that U999 will play a crucial role in Germany's future. And you, Leutnant, will have your part to play. Your dedication has already won you the Iron Cross; you can now prove that you are worthy of further honours.
SCHLANGE:	(*sinking back in his chair, almost at a loss for words*) Ach! (*Pauses.*) I knew it, during all those hard, bitter years at sea. Admiral, I will not falter in my determination to serve my Fuhrer and Reich.
SCHLEIM:	(*smiling and rising to shake hands with SCHLANGE*) I am sure of that. Now return to your ship, and good luck.
SCHLANGE:	(*rising to salute SCHLEIM and AUTOTREPPEN*) Heil Hitler!

SCHLEIM and AUTOTREPPEN: (*standing and saluting in response*) Heil Hitler!
ALL THREE: (*turning to the portrait and saluting*) Heil Hitler!
SCHLANGE turns and walks smartly from the room. His face bears the exalted expression of a man who is conscious of his great destiny.

Act 7

8 am, May 8th 1945. The control-room of U999, three miles off the German North Sea coast. As the ship is submerged and stationary, there is no sound, and the backdrop is grey. STOLLEN is seated and MULLER is standing nearby. SCHMIDT is in his cubicle. SCHLANGE is at the periscope.

STOLLEN: Anything, Snake?

SCHLANGE: Not a thing, Kapitan. Just grey sky, waves and seagulls.

STOLLEN: Watch the skies. If the Tommies come with their rocket-firing Typhoons or Sunderland flying-boats with depth-charges, we will not even start our secret mission. (*To MULLER*) Can you tell us anything, Leutnant?

MULLER: Only what Naval Intelligence in Flensburg told me. We were to sail to this point, and to be ready to receive a party and sealed orders.

STOLLEN: How long can this go on? The Fuhrer is dead, and most of the country is occupied.

SCHLANGE: Kapitan, last night I dreamed of this mission. I am sure it will be an epic, a day in which will sown the seeds of the greatest triumph in the history of the Reich.

STOLLEN: Well, don't dream now. Keep on sweeping the periscope around.

SCHLANGE: Jawohl (*breaks off.*) Kapitan!

STOLLEN: Yes?

SCHLANGE: Something on the horizon.

STOLLEN: Get up top with your binoculars. Surface, Schmidt!

SCHMIDT: Surface it is, Kapitan.

(*SCHLANGE exits up the conning tower ladder.*)

SCHLANGE: (*offstage*) Something coming up fast from abaft, sir. On the port quarter. It doesn't look very big.

STOLLEN: They can't radio to us in case the British pick up the signal. It could be an enemy warship. (Briskly) Make ready to dive.

SCHMIDT: Ready to dive it is, Kapitan.

SCHLANGE: Looks like a patrol-boat, sir; one of ours. She's getting quite close. Wait: they are flashing a signal-light. They are signalling, "Victory".

MULLER: That is the code-word. (*To STOLLEN*) Permission to signal back, Kapitan.

STOLLEN: Go ahead.

MULLER: Signal, "Vee".

SCHLANGE: (*after a pause*) I have done so. She is a patrol-boat, flying our colours. I estimate two minutes to come alongside.

Pause.

SCHLANGE comes backwards down the conning-tower ladder, followed by a figure in German naval uniform, who stands with his back partly turned so that his face can not be seen. Next comes a stooped figure in a great-coat and peaked cap. He too averts his face. Finally there emerges a fourth, uniformed figure, who turns, and is seen to be a strikingly attractive, blond woman. SCHLANGE gasps. The stooped figure slowly half-turns, revealing the lined and weary but unmistakable features of ADOLF HITLER. He then straightens up; his features

60

become stronger and more youthful. The actor is assuming the strength and charisma of the Fuhrer in, for him, more fortunate times.
SCHLANGE: (*awestruck*) Der Fuhrer! And Eva Braun!
STOLLEN: Der Fuhrer!
MULLER: Der Fuhrer!
ALL THREE: (*almost unbelieving*) Der Fuhrer!
All three stand as though thunderstruck, then SCHLANGE comes smartly to attention, clicking his heels and giving the Nazi salute. STOLLEN and MULLER follow suit.
ALL THREE: Heil Hitler!
HITLER returns the salute, then resumes his stoop, and, shepherded by the unidentified man, he shuffles off with EVA BRAUN through the door to the forward part of the ship. bulkhead doorway. In the doorway, the unidentified man turns. It is CAPTAIN CARSTAIRS.
MULLER: (*astonished*) You!
CARSTAIRS: (*in heavy, stage-German accent*) On the contrary, it is I. (*He gestures with his pistol at MULLER.*) Up--up! (*MULLER raises his hands.*)
CARSTAIRS: (*mockingly*) Ay--ay--ay--ay--ay--I like you vairee much. (*He laughs softly.*) When I'm calling you--oo--oo--oo--oo--oo--oo.
MULLER, with hands raised, regards him in consternation; STOLLEN gazes open-mouthed in disbelief at MULLER, and SCHLANGE grins delightedly.
CARSTAIRS: (*smiling*) Agent U, known also as Lieutenant Miller, of the British Secret Service, I place you under arrest.
MULLER: (*with feeling*) You traitor.
CARSTAIRS: No, my real name, as Snake will confirm, is Autotreppen. Hauptmann Autotreppen of German Naval Intelligence, to be precise, now revealed in my true colours as a loyal servant of the Reich.
STOLLEN: (*gazing stunned at MULLER*) I never once suspected (faltering) but where are my sealed orders?
CARSTAIRS: (*patting a bulge under his jacket*) I will let you have them just as soon as I have put this spy (*motions to MULLER.*) under lock and key, and made our Fuhrer comfortable.
SCHLANGE: It is all unfolding, just as in my dream. This is a great day for Germany.
CARSTAIRS: Set a course south-west for South America, where our Fuhrer will continue to lead and direct the struggle. (*He urges MULLER to the door and pushes him through.*)
Pause.
STOLLEN: I still can hardly believe it. Two years with a spy in our midst, and to think, I trusted him and regarded him as my (*hesitates.*) friend. (*He puts his hand to his eyes.*) Damn the war!
SCHLANGE: (*laughing openly*) I hope we shoot him soon, after we have tortured him to find out what he knows.
STOLLEN: (*coldly furious*) Dummkopf! As we speak, our last few redoubts are being overrun by the Allies. Most of your comrades in the U-boat service have been draughted into the army and at this moment are dying as cannon-fodder. If you ever get back to Germany you'll find the cities are heaps of rubble, and they'll

bang you into a prison-camp.

SCHLANGE: (*taken aback*) I---

The forward door opens with a loud clang and CARSTAIRS enters, closely followed by MULLER. Both have levelled pistols.

CARSTAIRS: (*speaking with an English accent*) One move and you're dead.

MULLER: He means it, Kapitan.

STOLLEN: (*making no move*) What is this? Why are you pointing that gun at me?

CARSTAIRS: Because, Kapitan, I am taking command of U999 in the name of the British Government. I am Captain Carstairs of British Naval Intelligence. (*He motions with the pistol.*) Take her down to ten fathoms.

STOLLEN: Watch where you are aiming that thing. The steel hull is pretty thin and rusty, and, if you miss me and put a hole in it, you'll (*pauses, at a loss for words.*) you'll answer to the Director of Operations in Cuxhaven.

CARSTAIRS: (*pained*) Kapitan, we have had enough stupid jokes already.

SCHLANGE nods emphatically.

CARSTAIRS: (*motioning again with his pistol*) Take it down or I will shoot!

STOLLEN: Go ahead then; shoot.

CARSTAIRS: (*breathing hard*) Kapitan, let me explain. Today is May 8th, 1945. Field Marshall Montgomery will shortly accept the unconditional surrender of the German forces in north western Europe, to be followed by formal surrender to General Eisenhower and Field Marshall Zhukov. The war is over.

STOLLEN: Not yet.

CARSTAIRS: Take her down. I don't want one of your patrol-boats sinking us now.

STOLLEN: (*calmly*) Go ahead and shoot. I accept orders only from the German High Command---

SCHLANGE: (*defiantly*) That goes for me as well.

STOLLEN: You will not find one man on this ship who will help you, and you cannot control it on your own. So go ahead and shoot.

The characters "freeze" in confrontational poses. Faintly, off-stage, a choir sings the Horst Wessel song. After a short while the set "comes to life" again.

MULLER: I can handle it. (*He shouts.*) Get out here , Schmidt.

SCHMIDT: (*from cubicle*) Kapitan?

MULLER strides into the cubicle. A moment later SCHMIDT stumbles out.

MULLER: Ready to take her down, Captain

Keeping his gun trained on STOLLEN, CARSTAIRS lowers the periscope. The backdrop darkens.

CARSTAIRS: Take---

RADIO OPERATOR: Kapitan, important bulletin coming through.

CARSTAIRS: (*to MULLER*) Wait. (*He motions to STOLLEN.*)

STOLLEN: Broadcast it.

There is a crackle of static, then the call-sign, Deutschland uber Alles, is played twice.

SOLEMN VOICE: Hier ist Flensburger Rundfunk. Our Fuhrer, Grand Admiral Karl Donitz, has announced the unconditional surrender of the German nation. All acts of war and resistance by our armed forces and civilians will cease immediately, and co-operation with the Allied forces is ordered. Grand Admiral Donitz will address the nation this afternoon at three o'clock.

All look grave. SCHLANGE is disbelieving.

STOLLEN: (*resignedly*) The war is over. Get back to your station, Schmidt. We will all obey Captain Carstairs' orders.

SCHMIDT: Jawohl, Kapitan. (*He goes back into his cubicle as MULLER emerges.*)

CARSTAIRS: Take her down to periscope depth.

STOLLEN: Periscope depth.

SCHMIDT: Periscope depth it is, Kapitan.

The backdrop slowly lightens, and the silhouette of a large warship is revealed. CARSTAIRS raises the periscope.

CARSTAIRS: (*peering intently through the periscope*) Right on time. The Duke of Cornwall with cruiser and destroyer escort. We are to convey Adolf Hitler into the custody of His Majesty's armed forces.

SCHLANGE: (*as though emerging from a trance*) Germany does not surrender. (*He grasps the firing-lever and pulls it.*) Fire one!

There is a muffled explosion. STOLLEN lunges at SCHLANGE and fells him with a violent blow.

STOLLEN: Are you deaf or stupid? The war is over! (*He pauses and looks puzzled.*) It seems to have misfired.

CARSTAIRS: (*to SCHLANGE, who is barely conscious*) You have just killed your Fuhrer. He was sheltering in number one torpedo-tube; he said it reminded him of his Berlin bunker, and he felt secure there. (*SCHLANGE slumps into unconsciousness.*)

CARSTAIRS: Surface!

STOLLEN: Surface!

SCHMIDT: Surface it is, Kapitan!

MULLER: (*softly*) Kapitan.

The stage goes quiet, and the light gradually fades. Faintly, a pale-rose spotlight shines on MULLER, then grows in brightness. Slowly and very gracefully, MULLER removes his cap, revealing lustrous, black curls, which spill gently downwards. A pale-blue spotlight then shines on STOLLEN, who moves slowly towards MULLER.

STOLLEN: (*whispering*) Leutnant, can this be true? (*The spotlights merge and then alternate in poignant, dappled rose and blue hues.*)

MULLER: (*tenderly*) Indeed it is, Kapitan.

They stare at each other as though hypnotised: faintly the music of There'll Be Bluebirds over, the White Cliffs of Dover begins.

STOLLEN: I never once suspected. But, then, I am stupid.

MULLER: (*laughing softly*) Yes, but in a very nice way.

They embrace. The spotlight becomes less intense, and changes to misty white. Slowly, with great tenderness, they kiss. The music fades.

STOLLEN: Liebchen.

MULLER: Dearest.

STOLLEN: In all these months you were never once out of my thoughts. The long hours on watch, endlessly gazing at grey seas and skies, and thinking, always thinking. The restless nights, and,

	when I did sleep, your face haunted my dreams; my heart pounding so loudly---
MULLER:	I could hear it; I used to think it was the diesels.
STOLLEN:	My every thought was you. Whenever we were torpedo-laying, raising the standard, dry-docking---
MULLER:	(*mischievously*) Wet-docking? (*They laugh and kiss again.*)
STOLLEN:	I don't even know your name; your real name.
MULLER:	Jenny Miller.
STOLLEN:	A beautiful name.
MULLER:	When I joined the Royal Navy, my family started to call me Jenny Wren.
STOLLEN:	That is beautiful too. I shall call you Jenny Wren.
MULLER:	But what is yours?
STOLLEN:	I never want to admit this. It is Adolf.
MULLER:	I can see why, but you are not like him. You are a kind, brave and considerate man. I am sure a lot of girls would have fallen for you, had you not been stuck on this tin-can.
STOLLEN:	(*laughing in mock-outrage*) Tin-can! I love this ship.
MULLER:	And I have learned to love it too. (*Adoringly*) As I have loved you intensely, from the moment I met you on the quayside at Cuxhaven. I longed to tell you how I felt, but how could I? We were sworn enemies. I hated lying to you; inventing that story about the cat's spying and stealing the fish, but there was no alternative.
STOLLEN:	Yes, I smelt a rat there.
MULLER:	Like the cat.
STOLLEN:	I thought it very improbable that the cat would steal fish. He knew that all he had to do was to come and ask. (*Reflectively*) Whenever I looked at you, through the engine row, I seemed to hear the chime of mountain bells, before the early morning mists have cleared. (*They kiss again, and bells chime faintly.*)
STOLLEN:	We must make plans for our life together. There's a beautiful little Alpine town called Mittenwald. We'll get a cottage there.
MULLER:	I can just picture it. (*Sentimentally*) I am sure it will be just like Bootle.
STOLLEN:	Really, it doesn't matter. We can live anywhere, even on (*pauses---*)
TOGETHER:	A submarine. (*They laugh.*)

The light extends throughout the stage. CARSTAIRS has turned from the periscope, and is watching with an approving smile.

| CARSTAIRS: | (*tactfully*) We had better make contact with Cornwall. |

The forward door opens and EVA BRAUN walks in unhurriedly. She has removed her greatcoat, and is wearing a plain, pale-blue, linen dress, which complements her blond hair. She is composed and dignified, and bears a faint smile. The orchestral strains of the music, Ding-dong, the Witch is Dead, are heard faintly and briefly.

STOLLEN:	(*coming to attention, respectfully*) Fraulein Braun.
BRAUN:	(*quietly*) I am Frau Hitler.
STOLLEN:	I am sorry. (*CARSTAIRS and MULLER look on silently and sympathetically.*)

SCHLANGE opens his eyes and gets unsteadily to his feet. Blood is pouring from his mouth. He has drawn his pistol, which he levels at CARSTAIRS.

SCHLANGE: (*to CARSTAIRS*) Get away from that! (*He gestures at the periscope*). (*CARSTAIRS makes no move.*)

SCHLANGE: (*grasping the torpedo firing-lever*) This German does not surrender. (*He pulls the lever.*) Fire two--- (*He pulls it again.*) Fire three. (*There are two muffled explosions. SCHLANGE sags weakly and drops his pistol.*)

There are two loud shots; CARSTAIRS shoots SCHLANGE, whose body jerks violently backward at each impact. He slumps to the deck, his right arm raised in the Nazi salute.

STOLLEN, MULLER and CARSTAIRS gaze in horror at SCHLANGE.

STOLLEN: (*slowly*) He died for what he believed in. He was no coward. (*He comes suddenly to life.*) Himmel! (*He dives to the periscope. Two loud explosions, and orange flashes on the waterline of the Duke of Cornwall.*)

STOLLEN: (*groaning*) Two direct hits. (*Flashes from the battleship's forward and after guns.*) They're firing back! Shouting: Dive-- dive--dive!

The klaxon screeches, then there is a deafening explosion, followed by a blinding, white flash. More explosions follow, with alternating blackness and vivid flashes of orange, blue and green. With each flash the occupants of the control-room are shown stroboscopically in various attitudes as they are violently buffeted around. Then there is darkness and silence.

Very slowly and gradually light returns to the stage. The control-room is badly damaged; smoke hangs in the air, there are several small fires, and sea-water is gushing in at various points. CARSTAIRS has been flung to the left of the room, and is sitting with his back to a bulkhead and his head sagging. His shirt is bloody. SCHMIDT has been ejected from the cubicle and is folded across a locker. SCHLANGE is slumped on the deck with his back resting against a console, his right arm raised in salute. EVA BRAUN is lying on her back with her legs apart (signifying the rape of a nation) and pointing towards the audience. Her arms are above her head. Her mouth is open and her eyes gaze sightlessly upwards. STOLLEN is lying face-down on MULLER, whose arms are around him.

Above them the Duke of Cornwall is well-ablaze along its entire length. Abruptly the stage is plunged into darkness. The loud strains of Hail the Conquering Hero, played flamboyantly by a military band, blare forth.

The End

SETS

THE CONTROL-ROOM OF U999.
This can be simple or elaborate, as decided by the Director, and as dictated by budgetary limits. To the right is Leutnant Muller's cabin.

THE LOUNGE OF THE U-BOAT OFFICERS' HOME IN CUXHAVEN.
This is comfortable and homely, and is simple or elaborate in design, as required.

"O"; HIS OFFICE IN NAVAL INTELLIGENCE, LONDON.
The style and furnishings should reflect the high rank of Commander Morrison.

REAR-ADMIRAL SCHLEIM'S OFFICE IN NAVAL INTELLIGENCE, BERLIN.
This is similar in concept to that of "O". An important feature is the dominating portrait of Adolf Hitler.

SOUND AND VISUAL EFFECTS

The backdrop is used to portray images of ships. These can be silhouettes in a night or misty setting, for warships, or, for the armed merchant-ship, Caramba, a detailed, coloured depiction may be prepared.

Vivid flashes in various colours are required for gunfire and torpedo sequences, accompanied by realistic noises of explosions. Stroboscopic imagery is required for the final act.

The sounds of the wind and sea, ship's sirens and klaxons, and machinery are extensively employed.

A selection of popular music of the late 'thirties and 'forties should precede the show, including the lighthearted, Artie Shaw version of Indian Love Call, Carmen Miranda's Ay--ay--ay--ay--ay--I Like You Vairee Much, Vera Lynn's There'll Be bluebirds Over…, and the Horst Wessel Song.

ACCENTS, VOCABULARY AND PRONUNCIATION

Comic stage-German should be employed sparingly, and only when a highly emphasised effect is required. Otherwise a slightly stilted, standard English accent is recommended.

The following German words are used.

Leutnant	loytnant.
Muller	u as in the French "tu".
Gott im Himmel	God in Heaven.
Kapitan	kapitaine.
Dummkopf	blockhead.
Fuhrer	u as in Muller. The u, in Muller and Fuhrer, correctly has an umlaut, as does the a in Kapitan, or are spelled ue and ae, respectively. Here, for simplicity, u and a are used on their own.
Schweinhund	shfinehoont. A very abusive word; literally "pig-dog", but actually untranslatable.
Schinkenwurst	shinkenvoorst - ham sausage
Reeperbahn	raperbarn.- "Ropemakers' Way"; a street in Hamburg.
Toast	toast.
Prosit!	prozit. - Toast!
Ko(e)nigsberg	kurnigsberg.
Guten Abend	Good evening.
Eva Braun	ayva brown.
Schleim	shlime.
Herein	herr-ine - come in.
Schnell	shnell - quickly.
Jawohl	yavole - yes, sir.
Was?	vass - what?
Was ist los?	vass ist loess - what is wrong?
Verdammt	ferdamt - damned.
Ach so	ak zoe - I see.
Bockwurst	bokvoorst - boiling sausage.
Liebchen	leepshen (glottal stop) - little love.
Kriegsmarine	German military navy.

OTHER PLAYS PUBLISHED BY
SILVERMOON PUBLISHING

Flushed
by Ron Nicol
(3f)
It's a singles night, and Jan and Meg are taking a break in the Ladies Room. Jan is criticising Tara, unaware that Tara is hiding in one of the toilet cubicles. When Tara's presence is revealed a fight ensues and Jan confesses the reason for her jealousy. Then Meg discovers that the door to the room seems to be locked, and the succeeding series of mishaps and misfortunes ruins Jan's appearance and assurance. Tara eventually manages to open the door, but on the threshold of escape they find that Meg is trapped in one of the cubicles.

The Beginner's Guide To Murdering Your Husband
or (Ten Easy Steps To Becoming A Widow)
Unwisely written by David Muncaster
(3f,2m)
This play is presented as though it is an instructional video that the audience are watching being filmed. Maddy will present a variety of methods for disposing of an unwanted husband, aided by Jim, her real life husband, and her faithful employees. But is she really trying to get rid of her husband? Is the video just a ruse to lull him into a false sense of security? The parallels with their real life relationship give Jim plenty to worry about but, as the play reaches its its climax, we realise that nothing is what it seems. Criss-cross indeed!

The World and its Arse
by David Muncaster
(6m,6f)
Frank's mind plays tricks on him as horrors from his past torment him. Len has nothing but memories. Brian doesn't know what he's got. He probably shouldn't even be there but he has nowhere else to go. A few days in an NHS ward give us a glimpse into the lives of a diverse set of people.

You see all sorts in here
Any colour, any class, any religion
Disease doesn't discriminate
You get the world and its arse come through that door

I Gave You My Heart
by David Muncaster
(2f)
Kate has received a parcel through the post from her ex-boyfriend. Her sister, Jenny thinks it is sweet, sending her a nice little parting gift. But Dan isn't sweet according to Kate. He's a freak, a weirdo. And whatever is in that box is somehow related to the last thing that he wrote on Kate's Facebook page – "I gave you my heart"

Nativity
by Jonathan Hall
(2m, 3f)
It's December 1979 and class 2G are getting ready for the school Nativity. Gemma wants to be Mary but because she's got a big loud voice she's the narrator, and anyway Sarah her best friend is far loads prettier than her, everyone says so. And as for Kirsty- she doesn't even get a look in, not that she cares, she's bothered about showing her knickers in the practical area. And of course there can only be one choice for Joseph, and that'd have to be Tony, everyone's favourite, complete with his thirteen colour biro. And Nicholas? In love with Sarah and dreams of flying through the milky way with her in the TARDIS? He's always going to be the Innkeeper.

Nativity is about the play we've all been in. About tea towels on heads and coconut-shell donkey hooves. Dinner ladies and toilet roll angels, reading books and Blue Peter. It's about our six year old selves, the adults that shaped us, the dreams that lit our days- and the people we have become.

Looking For Love
Raymond Hopkins
(4m,5f)
After twenty-one years of marriage, James Beale walks out on his wife, Molly. She is devastated and after four months of being alone, she has reached rock bottom. Her best friend, Fiona, persuades her to try the "six-step miracle cure" for abandoned wives. The idea being, on completion, she will be guaranteed to get her life back together. Molly agrees and finds that it works. Not only does her husband want to come back, but she has two other suitors vying for her affection. The twists and turns, the intrigues, the misunderstandings on her road to recovery, all add up to a hilarious evening's entertainment.

According To Claudia
Phil Mansell
(4f 3m)
This play is about the secrets that emerge when a family gathers to celebrate the 80th birthday of a crusty Oxford don. His daughters add fuel to the fire by bringing along partners who include a confused crime writer and a former gangster returning from the Costa del Crime. Mix in a dotty maiden aunt, a sad spinster and a mystery gunman and it adds up to a birthday party none of them will forget.

Splits In The Skin
Ron Nicol
(4f,2m)
The Dunstans meet for a rare family reunion at the request of their father, now aged 80. During an afternoon fraught with accusations, arguments, regrets and recriminations they look back on their childhood, reveal their best-kept secrets and deal with their father's unexpected and suspicious death.

Agatha Crusty And The Murder Mystery Dinner
Derek Webb
(5m, 6f)
Geoffrey and Caroline Robertson are having a dinner party to celebrate ten successful years of Mighty Midget Vacuum Cleaners, the company he jointly owns with Tim McArthur, and to add spice to the evening they decide to make it a murder mystery dinner. They are joined by a variety of employees and their partners. And Geoffrey has a special surprise – he has invited the well-known crime novelist Agatha Crusty (pronounced Croosty) to join them. She is in the area promoting her latest book and agrees to be guest of honour.

But on the evening of the dinner, their remote Victorian house finds itself in the centre of a storm so bad that the river floods and they are cut off. Worse, the power fails and in the darkness one of the guests is murdered. But since everybody else was together when the murder was committed, they are as perplexed as they are worried. And when another murder happens in the same way it is no laughing matter... except this is an Agatha Crusty murder mystery so there are laughs a-plenty. And also a genuine mystery that will keep an audience guessing as well as laughing.

Visit our website www.silvermoonpublishing.co.uk for regular updates to our catalogue